Let's Make Tudor Music

Contriv'd by
Lucie and Roddy Skeaping

*23 themed classroom projects
for Key Stage 2 Music*

First published in 1998 in Great Britain by
Stainer & Bell Ltd, 23 Gruneisen Road, London N3 1DZ
Reprinted 2002
Produced in association with the Early Music Network

© 1998 Stainer & Bell Ltd

All rights reserved. This book is copyright under the
Berne Convention. It is fully protected by the British
Copyright, Designs and Patents Act 1988. No part of this
publication may be reproduced, stored in a retrieval system,
or transmitted in any form or by any means, electronic,
mechanical, photocopying, recording or otherwise without
the prior permission of Stainer & Bell Ltd.

British Library Catalogue-in-Publication Data
A catalogue record of this book is available from the British Library

Teacher's Book (including CD): ISBN 0 85249 847 0
Pupil's Book (available in packs of 10 copies): ISBN 0 85249 848 9

The cover photograph, by Rory Carnegie,
shows the authors (centre), with their
group The City Waites.

The photograph on page 33 is used by permission
of Shakespeare's Globe and Pentagram Design Ltd.

The photograph on page 51 is used by permission
of the Mary Rose Trust.

Printed in Great Britain by Caligraving Ltd
Typeset by Silverfen

About the Authors

Early music has always been the compelling enthusiasm of Lucie and Roddy Skeaping, a husband-and-wife team whose diversity of talents as singers, instrumentalists, teachers, scholars and animateurs has, for many years, placed them at the forefront of British musical life.

Deeply committed to the revival of the Medieval, Renaissance and Baroque repertoires, they have specialised in the reconstruction of early English popular music, playing period instruments in authentic performances given by their own ensemble, *The City Waites*. Their celebrated workshops for schools, *The Musical Mystery Tour*, and their many CDs, have introduced early music to young audiences throughout much of Europe, the USA and the Far East. In addition, with their ensemble *The Burning Bush*, they have extended their pursuit of authenticity into the colourful world of Jewish folk music.

Both Lucie and Roddy Skeaping trained at the Royal College of Music, where Roddy subsequently returned to teach viola da gamba and later as a Leverhulme Research Fellow. Alongside his large teaching practice he is also a versatile composer for choirs and chamber ensembles. His work has taken him into theatre and television as a composer and musical director for the Royal National Theatre, Shakespeare's Globe Theatre, the Young National Trust Theatre Company and the Royal Shakespeare Company. Lucie is also a frequent broadcaster, presenting children's and schools' programmes both for BBC radio and television, as well as many mainstream series and features on early and traditional music.

Quick reference guide to contents

Title	Singing	Playing instruments	Composing/ improvising	Drama	Dance	CDT	Page
Fanfare		✓	✓	✓		✓	10
Martin said to his Man	✓		✓	✓			14
A Royal Banquet	✓	✓		✓	✓		16
Street Cries	✓	✓	✓	✓			18
The Song of the Cutpurse	✓	✓		✓			22
The Tale of Sir Eglamore and the Dragon	✓	✓		✓		✓	24
When that I was a Little Tiny Boy	✓	✓		✓			30
Henry VIII's Song	✓	✓	✓				34
Katherine of Aragon's Song	✓	✓					36
Anne Boleyn's Song	✓	✓	✓				40
Jane Seymour's Tune		✓	✓				42
Anne of Cleves' Dance		✓	✓		✓		44
Catherine Howard's Song	✓	✓					46
A Sailor's Dance for Catherine Parr		✓	✓				48
Tomorrow the Fox will come to Town	✓	✓	✓				52
Robin Hood and the Poacher	✓	✓	✓	✓			54
Three Blind Mice	✓		✓				58
Eliza is the Fairest Queen	✓	✓		✓	✓		62
Queen Elizabeth's Almain					✓		66
Long Live Fair Oriana	✓						70
The Death of Queen Elizabeth				✓			72
The Invincible Armada	✓	✓	✓	✓		✓	76
The Spanish Pavan		✓			✓		82

Contents and CD track list

Preface — 6
Introduction — 8

TUDOR BANQUET
Fanfare — CD track [1] and [2] — 10
Martin said to his Man — [3] and [4] — 14
A Royal Banquet — 16

TUDOR TOWN LIFE
Street Cries — [5] and [6] — 18
The Song of the Cutpurse — [7] — 22
The Tale of Sir Eglamore and the Dragon — [8] — 24
When that I was a Little Tiny Boy — [9] — 30

HENRY VIII AND HIS SIX WIVES
Henry VIII's Song — [10] and [11] — 34
Katherine of Aragon's Song — [12] and [13] — 36
Anne Boleyn's Song — [14] — 40
Jane Seymour's Tune — [15] and [16] — 42
Anne of Cleves' Dance — [17] and [18] — 44
Catherine Howard's Song — [19] and [20] — 46
A Sailor's Dance for Catherine Parr — [21] and [22] — 48

TUDOR SPORTS AND PASTIMES
Tomorrow the Fox will come to Town — [23] and [24] — 52
Robin Hood and the Poacher — [25] — 54
Three Blind Mice — [26] and [27] — 58

QUEEN ELIZABETH I
Eliza is the Fairest Queen — [28] and [29] — 62
Queen Elizabeth's Almain — [30] — 66
Long Live Fair Oriana — [31] — 70
The Death of Queen Elizabeth — [32] — 72

SIR FRANCIS DRAKE AND THE ARMADA
The Invincible Armada — [33] — 76
The Spanish Pavan — [34] and [35] — 82

Glossary of instruments — 84

Preface

From the very beginnings of the National Curriculum Music Working Group, we determined to make proposals which ensured that Music should be an active, participatory subject. We were fortunate that much thinking had taken place in the preceding decade: already, the notion of passive 'Music Appreciation' was outdated, and the three activities - performing, composing and listening - had been clearly defined. Not that 'knowledge' is irrelevant - to know the mechanics of an instrument may explain why it sounds as it does; to know the social context of a dance may give vital clues about how to play it. But such factual information is not, in itself, 'musical' until it impinges on one or more of the activities.

We were also determined that the Music curriculum should be as flexible as possible. In some respects it is strongly prescriptive. Pupils *must* gain experience of folk and popular music, of music of the European 'classical' tradition, of other cultures, from the countries and regions of the British Isles, and from well-known composers and performers, past and present. But we did not specify a single composer, a single performer, a single work. That was left to teachers, recognising their professional role and capitalising on particular enthusiasms, opportunities and local circumstances.

We were also confident that music had a particularly important part to play within the wider curriculum. Choosing and evaluating words and reflecting their rhythms in composing are invaluable spurs to literacy; singing and chanting are powerful aids to learning - mathematical tables for example; songs and musical styles encompass history and geography; the Science curriculum includes specific music-related requirements; music is deeply embedded in religious ceremony.

All this clarified and strengthened the role of Music as a component of the curriculum. But, while it left teachers with great freedom, it also imposed on them a heavy responsibility. Specialists at Key Stage 3 could manage this: 'generalist' teachers at the earlier Key Stages could find it daunting. We were determined, however, to propose the kind of curriculum which pupils deserved rather than water-down its requirements to what every school could cope with. We envisaged two strategies: in-service training such as had taken much of the threat from the demands of the Science curriculum and the provision of teaching/learning materials which could allow any teacher, however 'unmusical' they may believe themselves to be, to enable pupils to be active musicians.

Let's Make Tudor Music is a remarkable example of such provision. It takes one of the curriculum 'themes', and enhances it by investigating Tudor food, street markets, crime, theatre, sea-faring, and the manners, sports and pastimes of Henry's and Elizabeth's court. It draws pupils into listening and appraising - a critical, responsive approach to what is heard. They immediately perform - real music rather than *ersatz* alternatives. Then, they are invited to improvise, compose and arrange their own musical reflections on facets of Tudor life.

The authors combine musical professionalism with sensitivity both *as* teachers themselves and *to* their unknown colleagues in the classroom - a rare mix, and one which teachers will find deeply reassuring. Vocal ranges are carefully selected, and the slow-tempo CD 'Learning Tracks' are the simplest of strategies. The recorded performances are full of imagination and commitment, for example the crumhorn virtuosity in *Pastime with Good Company*. Yet, while the musical fare is uncompromisingly professional, teachers have to hand all the material they need to engage pupils in it to a very high level of achievement. Subjects are suggested for 'appraising'; all pitches are provided; everything is demonstrated in sound; there is a simple teaching methodology for dance (clearly borrowed from Victor Silvester!).

Stainer & Bell's initiative, realised by the inspiration of the two authors, has produced a major collection of classroom material which fulfils not only the requirements of the Music curriculum at Key Stage 2, but reaches deeply into the heart of the wider curriculum. If, as is threatened as I write, the statutory requirements of many subjects including Music are lifted, the need for guidance becomes, paradoxically, even greater. On behalf of the Early Music Network, which has supported this project, I recommend it wholeheartedly and echo the authors' exhortation - have fun!

Professor George Pratt
April 1998

Introduction

Welcome to *Let's Make Tudor Music*. This Teacher's Book, with its accompanying Pupil's Book and CD, forms a unique concept in music education that enables you to meet many of the specific attainment targets contained in the National Curriculum for Key Stage Two Music, while exploring the riches of Tudor music through the exciting medium of classroom performance.

Let's Make Tudor Music is a new idea, but all the songs, instrumental pieces and other activities have been tried and tested over many years in our frequent visits to schools with our 'Musical Mystery Tour' workshops. The project also carries important cross-curricular links with History, English, Drama, Dance and CDT, embracing characters, events and themes with which pupils at this level will already be familiar.

Let's Make Tudor Music consists of a Teacher's Book, a Pupil's Book, and a specially recorded CD. The CD features complete performances of all the pieces, recorded by skilled early music performers. The parts that pupils learn to sing or play are woven into the musical texture, enabling them to join in the performance, playing along with the professional musicians on the CD. So don't worry if the instruments we suggest for any piece are not available in your particular class - the parts will still be there on the recording, and we'll literally be there on the disc, lending our support!

Let's Make Tudor Music has been created to adapt to a wide range of classroom situations. The ability to read music is not necessary for pupils (or teachers!) as most of the parts can be played by ear. You will find, however, that as pupils listen to the CD and become familiar with their music, they will naturally begin to interpret the simple note values and pitches they see on the page.

On the CD a particular piece is, in some cases, preceded by a **Learning Track** which isolates a special aspect of the piece in question. For more advanced pupils, or where the teacher can manage a simple guitar part, we have also included a few pieces that can be played without the CD.

Let's Make Tudor Music is not a progressive project - you can just dip in, or choose a piece which focuses on your class's particular skills, needs or interests. There are also some suggestions for linking sections together, and for adding drama or movement to make a short presentation. Each chapter follows a similar pattern, with the focus points clearly stated for ease of reference, and with a paragraph of useful information concerning the musical and historical background to the piece. The practical element then falls into three parts:

1 Listening and appraising

Pupils listen to the complete piece on the main CD track, and discuss it. These discussions can be guided by the points raised under *Things to talk about*, but pupils should also be encouraged to share their spontaneous responses to the music. Play the track many times, as new observations will be made on each occasion. For the first few times, pupils should listen only, their books closed. Then, encourage them to follow music and words as they listen, naming, from the front of the book, the featured instruments depicted on the appropriate page as a learning exercise.

2 Now - let's make Tudor music!

Here, the class divides into groups of instrumentalists and singers, each learning their parts separately. We suggest, however, that in the case of a song, everyone (including those who will subsequently choose to play an instrument) learns to sing the song together before the instruments are handed out. For some pieces, there is a **Learning Track** after the main CD track. Use both tracks as often as you like to help pupils learn their parts. Once everyone feels secure with their part, go for a 'performance', playing along with the main CD track.

3 Other things to try

This section contains suggestions for follow-up work related to composition, historical context, visual arts, and many other related aspects of Tudor music. For this part, teachers may wish to bring their own particular enthusiasms or interests to the classroom. There are also opportunities here to link up with other National Curriculum subjects, perhaps even involving the whole school.

In writing *Let's Make Tudor Music* we have tried to combine historical scholarship with a practical approach to what happens in the classroom. Here, in addition, are a few tips we recommend for getting the best from your music making:

- As the music is printed only in the Pupil's Book, teachers should have a copy of both the Teacher's and Pupil's Books open during the lesson.

- When pupils are asked to 'clap along with the CD', gentle one-fingered clapping (i.e. clapping with one finger on the palm of the hand) is best.

- When learning songs, pupils should follow these three steps before finally singing along with the performance on the CD:

    1 **Say** the words without the CD track to make sure they're understood.

    2 Say the words along with the CD track, **in rhythm**, to discover which syllable belongs to which note.

    3 **Hum** the tune (no words) along with the CD track.

- Some instrumental parts in the Pupil's Book are printed with the words of the song underneath. These words are not for the pupils playing the instruments to sing as well, but will help them to keep their place as they play.

- 'Recorder' always means descant recorder, unless specified otherwise.

- We have sometimes marked symbols (√) to show where to take a breath, but don't worry too much. Pupils should take breaths in the most natural place, though preferably not in the middle of a word or phrase!

- Whenever pupils are asked to improvise or compose, they should listen to each other's efforts and discuss the results - an important part of the creative process.

You will find *Let's Make Tudor Music* contains lots to learn, lots to do and lots to talk about. At whatever level your class is able to participate - have fun!

Lucie and Roddy Skeaping
April 1998

TUDOR BANQUET

Fanfare

— CD Tracks 1 and 2 —

FOCUS ON:
Music that has a function
Repeating note and rhythm patterns
Composing

This fanfare is taken from a popular Elizabethan dance tune called the Bergamesca.

Listening and appraising

You can hear: CORNETTOS, SACKBUTS, DRUMS

The piece is played three times round:
- *1st time* - the melody as written;
- *2nd time* - rhythmic variety in the wind instruments;
- *3rd time* - rhythmic variety in the drums.

Things to talk about

1 What is the function of a fanfare? *(to attract attention/to announce something important/for a procession)*

2 What instruments can you hear on the track and how are they played? *(blown, struck or plucked etc.)*

3 Can you tell when the piece starts again each time? *(pupils should raise their hands to indicate)*

4 Listen to the drum beat all through. What happens to it in the last verse? *(extra notes are added)*

5 Listen to the melody all through. What happens to it on the 2nd time round? *(extra notes are added)*

6 Look at the printed music in the Pupil's Book. Some notes have dots above or below them, others have dashes. How do they sound different?
(♩ = short and spikey,
  ♩ = smooth and flowing)

7 Identify repeating note patterns in the printed music. Point to any bars which look exactly the same. *(bars 1 and 3 are the same, and bars 5 and 7 are the same)*

8 Think of examples of modern fanfares. *(e.g. on a TV show after someone has won/entry of a new contestant)*

Now - let's make Tudor music!

RECORDERS/VIOLINS:
First, why not use the LEARNING TRACK (CD Track 2), which is slower.
Start playing after the drum introduction on the track. Try to copy both the *'spikey'* and the *'smooth'* ways of playing the notes (indicated by dots and dashes). Pupils should suggest their own rhythms for the 2nd time through.

DRUMS/TABORS:
First, why not use the LEARNING TRACK (CD Track 2), which is slower.
Start playing after the slow drum introduction on the track. Pupils should suggest different rhythms for the 3rd time through.

CHIME BARS/BASS XYLOPHONE/ CELLOS/OTHER LOW PITCH INSTRUMENTS:
You need notes G C D. Be sure to get the speed right - play *one* note to every *two* of the melody line. This part simply repeats a two-bar note pattern.

OTHER PUPILS:

- Imitate the *cornetto* (it plays the melody line/top line on the CD track), vocalising the melody down a large rolled-up piece of paper.

- Play a comb and tissue paper: fold the paper round a comb with the teeth pointing upwards, hold gently to mouth and hum the melody.

*As pupils gain confidence they may like to try performing the fanfare without the CD track. Divide RECORDERS/VIOLINS into two groups. One group plays the 'A' section and the other plays the 'B' section **at the same time**. Then swap parts. Other instruments can play the same parts as before.*

Compose your own fanfare

After pupils have played the Tudor fanfare they can try inventing their own. Divide into groups of three, each with recorder, percussion and chime bars represented in it.

- **Recorders/violins**: compose a fanfare, starting with a note pattern on G, then adding other notes.

- **Percussion players**: use varied rhythms, but steady as before.

- **Chime-bar players etc**: play the following repeated note-pattern: G G D G in that order.

Use repeated notes and rhythmic patterns like those you can hear on the CD, and try to use both *'short and spikey'* and *'smooth'* notes. It helps if the percussion starts, setting up a simple introductory rhythm. Listen to each other's compositions and then play them one after the other to make one long fanfare!

Other things to try

1 Discuss the MENU in the Pupil's Book. How does it differ from a normal 20th-century meal? Would pupils fancy eating a meal like this?

2 Divide the class into two groups, ideally with a selection of instruments in each. Each group chooses a dish from the MENU and finds its own way of performing a fanfare (either the Tudor fanfare or their original composition). Start with a short series of drum beats to attact attention. Then, loudly and clearly, one pupil from the group announces the name of the dish, and the group immediately follows with their music.

3 If space allows, as each fanfare is being performed, pupils who are not playing instruments could process through the room, walking in time to the beat, taking an imaginary dish towards an imaginary royal 'top table'. First of all, they could try guessing how many times round the music will need to be played to cover the length of the journey. Were they right?

TUDOR BANQUET

Martin said to his Man

— CD Tracks 3 and 4 —

FOCUS ON:
Singing, acting in character and creating lyrics
Distinguishing between verse and chorus

This is a popular drinking song by Elizabethan composer Thomas Ravenscroft. Originally a chorister at St Paul's Cathedral, he is better known for his church music, but he also wrote, arranged and published lots of popular songs.

Listening and appraising

You can hear: SINGERS

There are five verses.

Things to talk about

1. Why do the characters in the song see strange things? *(they're drunk!)* What's odd about the things they see?

2. Who is Martin's 'man'? *(his servant)*

3. What words do we use nowadays instead of 'Fie man'? *(nonsense!/don't be silly! etc.)*

4. What happens to the SPEED in the last verse? *(gets slower)* What MOOD does this create?

5. In verses 2, 3 and 4, can you tell when the solo singer is singing and when the chorus joins in? *(pupils should raise hands to indicate)* What happens in the first and last verses? *(everyone sings together all through)*

6. Look at the printed music in the Pupil's Book. Point to any bars that have the notes rising and falling in a similar PATTERN. *(the notes in bars 1 and 2 have a similar pattern to those in bars 3 and 4, but they are pitched a little lower)*

Now - let's make Tudor music!

SINGERS:
To help pick up the melody, why not use the LEARNING TRACK (CD Track 4), which has verse 1 sung slowly.

Everyone should learn the whole song first. Keep the words crisp, and watch out for the interval, in the last line each time between '(...drunken) man' and 'who's (the fool...)'

Now divide the class into three groups, each group taking the 'solo' phrases of each verse, and everyone else singing the chorus interjections. Pupils should respond to each other with vocal characterisation and mime. They can invent voices and movements to match the words of each verse - the funnier the better - but try to stay in tune!

You could also try giving out solos, with just one pupil singing the solo phrases, and with everyone else joining in the chorus interjections.

If everyone feels confident enough, try a performance without using the CD track. Get the starting note from chime-bar note G.

Other things to try

1 Divide the class into lots of small groups and make up your own 'strange visions' in the same 'I see...' format.

   For example:

   I see a boat in the air... and a cat with curly hair.

   Now try singing the whole song (without the CD track, of course) using the newly made-up verses, one after the other, but retaining the original chorus interjections.

2 Show the class the original printed page of this song (page 39). Can they read it? Discuss what early notation looked like compared with that in the Pupil's Book. Look at verse 2, which is not included in this book.

TUDOR BANQUET

A Royal Banquet
A short drama presentation

This scene links together the two pieces in the Tudor Banquet section, *Fanfare* (page 10) and *Martin said to his Man* (page 14) with *The Spanish Pavan* (page 82) and *Queen Elizabeth's Almain* (page 66).

Feel free to use the various CD tracks during this presentation. It might be a good idea to have someone ready by your CD player, whose job is to switch it on and off. Individual roles are chosen from the class, and the remaining pupils play the courtiers.

The cast:
    KING AND QUEEN
    MASTER OF CEREMONIES
    ROYAL FOOD TASTER
    MUSICIANS
    FOUR JESTERS
    COURTIERS
    CD-PLAYER OPERATOR

Props:
A large serving dish or tray (this could be an oval shape cut out of thick card and covered in tin foil) and 'food' to go on it. Try using a dark stocking stuffed with paper for meat, green tissue for lettuce, painted polystyrene for fish, etc.

THE PLAY

Music: *The Spanish Pavan*

The music is played as the courtiers arrive and, chatting quietly, take their seats at tables. Enter Master of Ceremonies, beating a drum to silence everyone (two or three strong beats will do). Music stops.

MASTER OF CEREMONIES   Your Royal Majesties, my Lords and Ladies, our cooks have this day prepared the finest, most flavoursome dish in England, the ... *(chooses something from menu).*

Music: FANFARE
This is played as the dish is paraded around the room and placed finally in front of the King, who, takes some food from the dish and puts it in his mouth.

QUEEN   Stop, My Lord! You know you must not eat anything until it has been tested - it may be poisoned!

COURTIERS   We agree/you must take care etc.

KING   How silly of me. Bring me my Royal Food Taster!

The Royal Food Taster nervously swallows the food. There is a dramatic silence...

COURTIERS	(*gasping*) Ooh!
ROYAL FOOD TASTER	I pronounce the food wholesome - and delicious!
COURTIERS	(*all cheer*)

Enter four Jesters, who address the King.

JESTER 1	We humbly crave your noble Majesty's ear to hear a song newly writ.
JESTER 2	It is upon the evil humours brought about by that most terrible of vices...
ALL JESTERS	...drink!
KING	We wish to hear this new song, pray sing it.

Music: *Martin said to his Man*

The four Jesters mime the actions as everyone sings the song.

COURTIERS	(*loud applause and laughter*)
KING	That was a truly wonderful banquet. Throw the leftovers to the peasants.
COURTIERS	Oh yes/what a good idea/we agree etc.
KING	Indeed it has put me in such a good mood that I bid you all join me in a dance.
COURTIERS	Oh yes/what a good idea/we agree etc.

The King and Queen rise and walk to centre of floor. The courtiers join them and take starting positions for the dance.

Music: *The Queen's Almain*

All dance

TUDOR TOWN LIFE

Street Cries

— CD Tracks 5 and 6 —

FOCUS ON:
Learning a short phrase and retaining it within a texture of sound
Improvising and composing sounds and structures to create an atmosphere

Street traders sang their 'cries' in cities and towns to advertise their wares and services. The song Brooms for Old Shoes - and the selection of individual street cries - are taken from works by Tudor composers who were inspired by their tuneful nature.

Listening and appraising

Use CD Track 5

You can hear: FOUR SINGERS
They start singing one after the other.

Things to talk about

1 Difficult words may be:
brooms	= shrubs used to sweeten the smell of old shoes
pouch rings	= leather ring to fasten a purse
buskins	= high leather boots
pippins	= a variety of apple
to cleave	= to chop up

2 The last singer to enter is not selling anything. Who is he? *(the nightwatchman telling the time)*

3 Looking at the words in the Pupil's Book, and listening, count how many different things are on offer.

4 How does the texture build up? *(singers enter one after the other until all four are singing together; pupils should raise their hands each time they hear a new voice added)*

5 Pupils should listen to one particular voice and follow it all the way through the increasingly complex texture of the song. How many times does each voice sing? *(voice 1 sings his part five times; voice 2 sings her part four times; voice 3: three times; voice 4: twice)*

Now - let's make Tudor music!

Use CD Track 6, which contains a selection of Street Cries for pupils to learn.

SINGERS:
You hear each cry sung four times, by both solo voice and chorus. Join in with the choruses using a good loud voice - you need to be heard at the other end of town!

CHIME-BAR DRONE PLAYERS:
This part is a repeated steady beat, using notes C and G played together. (You can hear it played on a lute on the CD track.)

Have as many goes through with this CD track as you like, stopping as you go to discuss what all the cries mean:

Seville oranges - from Spain
ends of gold or silver - for melting down
Kind-Heart - a painless dentist!

When pupils are familiar with the above, stop the CD and go on to **The Circle Game**.

The Circle Game:
In this game, pupils evoke the atmosphere of a Tudor street, starting in the early morning when things are quiet, and building up to a busy day's trading. It requires pupils to be creative, retain a short phrase at pitch, sing or play it as directed within the surrounding musical texture and respond to each other's performance.

You will need: One or two CHIME-BAR players, beating a steady drone as practised earlier. (Teachers who play the guitar can strum a chord of C to reinforce this.)

Another CHIME-BAR player (optional) making a 'church bell' effect by playing a descending scale (from high C to low C), repeating *ad libitum*.

One CONDUCTOR who directs and controls the shape of the piece, using simple signs.

The REST OF THE CLASS, divided into groups (up to four pupils in each). They decide, between themselves, which cry their group will sing (but avoid duplication between groups).

Positions: The groups who are going to 'cry' form a large circle. The CONDUCTOR and the CHIME-BAR players are placed in the middle.

To start: CHIME-BAR DRONE players start a slow, steady beat (about the same speed as the lute heard on the CD track) and keep going throughout the piece. The CONDUCTOR then points to one group of 'criers' who start to sing in time with the pulse. The CONDUCTOR can choose to keep the cries going

(repeating over and over) while
he starts another group, stopping
and starting them as he likes.

Shaping the piece: At any point in the piece there can be as
many or as few groups singing as the
CONDUCTOR chooses. He or she uses simple
signals, for example:

1) to *start* a particular group:
   Points at them

2) to *stop* a particular group:
   Points at them with palm of hand

3) to *change the volume* of a group:
   Points and raises or lowers arm

The whole piece doesn't need to
last more than a minute. Have lots
of goes, giving other pupils a turn
at being the CONDUCTOR.

Other things to try

Make up your own modern street cries. They could be similar to those still heard in markets today - or as crazy as you like!

Examples:

Come, buy my nice Ford Escort!

New computers for old!

Pink stripy T-shirts, come and try them on!

It is important that the rhythm of the cry should *follow the natural pattern of the words*, and that the phrases should be simple and catchy. Examples should be offered and discussed by the class and the most successful should be selected and sung by everyone. You may like to write down those that work best, using a system of words and symbols.

TUDOR TOWN LIFE

The Song of the Cutpurse

— CD Track 7 —

FOCUS ON:
Rhythmic patterns
Tudor punishments
Performance with reading

A cutpurse was a thief who cut the purses which were tied to people's belts. As this song shows, punishment for petty crime was often very harsh in Tudor times, and a public hanging was a frequent spectacle. This melody - the popular dance tune Packington's Pound - was used for a number of ballads, of which this is one.

Listening and appraising

You can hear: SINGER, BASS REBEC, DRUM

There is one verse which begins and ends with a four-bar drum pattern.

Things to talk about

1 What was a cutpurse - and what is today's equivalent? (*pickpocket, bag snatcher*)

2 Public hangings/gallows; were they a good thing? What is the punishment nowadays?

3 At the end of the song, the cutpurse gives advice to young people: 'Young friends...'

4 The bass rebec: talk about how it is played and describe its timbre? (*reedy*)

5 Talk about the MOOD of the song and what effect the slow speed and the drum beat has. (*the steady drum all through could represent the cutpurse's final walk to the gallows; the extra-loud last beat could represent his death*)

Now – let's make Tudor music!

SINGERS:
Speak the words first, along with the track, then sing with it as often as you need. Look out for the word 'hang-ed' near the end - it has two syllables. Singers should learn when to start by counting the four drum beats that precede their entry. Try to sing loud and strong, perhaps with a 'rough edge' to the voice, bearing in mind the mood of the text.

DRUMS (as large and deep as possible):
Look at the rhythmic pattern on the page: it has three slow beats plus two faster ones in the last bar. Clap it first, then try it out on instruments. As you play, it may help to repeat out loud 'One, two, three, four - and...', as printed above the notes. The drums start playing after the four drum beats on the CD track - first beat on the word 'masters'. Repeat the pattern throughout the song. At the end, don't forget to play the last beat - very loud!

As pupils gain confidence they may like to perform this song without the CD track. Take your first two starting notes from the chime bars: A followed by the D above. You can play through the drum pattern as many times as you like before the singers start.

Other things to try

You might like to precede a performance of *The Song of the Cutpurse* with the following reading (you can simplify or shorten it as appropriate for your class):

In Tudor times, pickpockets or cutpurses would sometimes gang-up with street musicians. For example, a rough singer would gather a crowd around him outdoors in the market square, and begin his song. After a few verses he would suddenly stop and shout to his audience: *'Ladies and gentlemen, check your purses - I hear there are cutpurses in the crowd today!'* Everyone would then feel for their purses and pat their clothes to check them, unaware that by this very act they were giving away, to the sharp-eyed cutpurses, the exact whereabouts of their valuables! The singer would then resume his song as the cunning thieves (who had arranged a deal with the singer) skillfully 'relieved' them of their most treasured items!

TUDOR TOWN LIFE

The Tale of Sir Eglamore and the Dragon

— CD Track 8 —

FOCUS ON:
Acting out a song

At various times of the year a town or city would play host to companies of travelling players, who would set up a pitch in the street, tavern, courtyard or market place and perform a play. They carried with them all the things they needed - costumes and props, even their own stage. The plays were often simple moral tales portraying the conflict between Good and Evil with acting, singing and dancing. This ballad still remains popular today as part of Britain's folk-song repertoire. The words describe the action vividly, and the song works well when acted out in traditional style.

Listening and appraising

You can hear: SINGERS, CITTERN, VIOLIN, CURTAL

There are six sung verses and three instrumental verses. The song starts with an instrumental verse.

Things to talk about

1. This sounds like a comic song to us nowadays. Do you think it was funny to a Tudor audience? Did people believe in dragons? Were they scared of them? Talk about the Knight and Dragon as symbols of Good and Evil.

2. Discuss any difficult words, such as:
    coat of mail = chain mail
    good lack = goodness me
    hilt = handle of a sword
    preserve = look after

3. Identify the instruments you can hear: the violin plays the melody, the cittern plays the plucked chord (a 'jangley', rhythmic part), and the curtal plays the bass line.

4 The MOOD of the song. Perhaps the 'swinging' rhythm is reminiscent of a galloping horse? And the simple catchy chorus helps create a light-hearted mood.

5 How many times does the chorus 'interject' in each verse? Talk about the difference between the three interjections. *(the third is longer)*

6 Look at the three chorus interjections in the Pupil's Book. In the first two, the notes start low and rise up before dropping down again.

7 Find words to describe the sound of the curtal. *(plays the bass notes)* Also talk about the function of a bass instrument in this context. *(to provide a solid harmonic and rhythmic anchor)*

8 Look for any repeated note patterns in the printed music. *(bars 1 and 2 are the same as bars 5 and 6)*

Now - let's make Tudor music!

SINGERS/RECORDERS:
First, say the words of the choruses a few times (they don't mean anything!). Then learn the chorus melody by singing along with the track. Then have a go at the verses too. When everyone feels confident, divide the class into two groups: singers and recorder players (their parts are exactly the same).
Don't forget - this song tells a story, so make sure the words are really clear.

CHIME BARS/BASS XYLOPHONE/CELLOS/OTHER LOW PITCHED INSTRUMENTS:
Isolate the notes G, C and D. You can use the song words, printed underneath, as a guide.

TEACHER'S GUITAR PART (optional):
Guitar chords are printed in the Pupil's Book. If you are able to provide a guitar accompaniment you might like to try performing this song without the CD. This will allow for more flexibility when you act it out.

Acting it out

Most classes will enjoy working out their own way of performing this song. Details of how to make costumes and props are found on page 28. Ask pupils for their ideas. Perhaps they will even have some suggestions for casting! Here are some basic ideas for performance:

THE CAST

SIR EGLAMORE
THE DRAGON
THE HILL
THE CAVE (2 people)
SINGERS

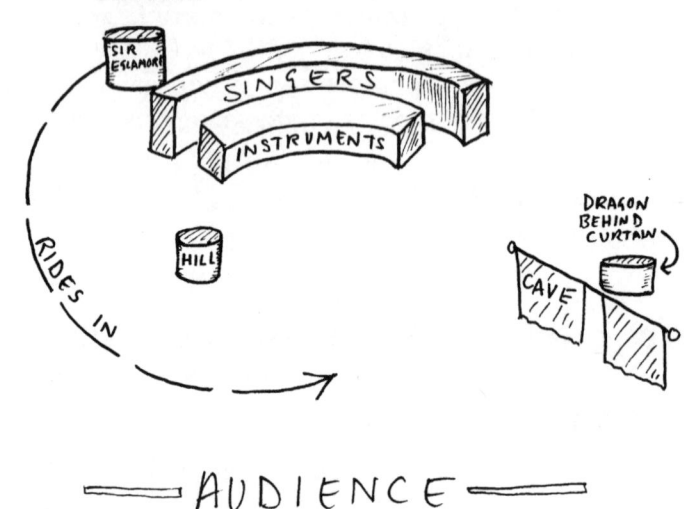

OPENING POSITIONS

SIR EGLAMORE	*waiting off stage*
THE DRAGON	*crouching behind the cave*
THE HILL	*seated on the floor in the middle of the performing area, near the front*
THE CAVE	*standing on the right, diagonally, near the front*
SINGERS	*seated on the left and right of performing area*

WORDS OF THE SONG	STAGE DIRECTIONS
INSTRUMENTAL VERSE	*Sir Eglamore gallops in from the opposite side from the cave.*
1. Sir Eglamore that valiant knight He fetched his sword and he went to fight, And as he rode o'er hill and dale All clothed in his coat of mail *With his fa, la, fa, la, lanky down dilly.*	*Sir Eglamore gallops around the stage, and rides over (or round) the hill.*
2. A huge great dragon leapt out of her den That had killed the Lord knows how many men, And when she saw Sir Eglamore Good lack had you heard how that dragon did roar!	*The dragon leaps out of her den. Sir Eglamore stops at the opposite side of the stage and looks around. The dragon flexes her muscles and points to Sir Eglamore. The dragon and singers give a loud roar. Sir Eglamore looks scared.*
3. The dragon's skin was tough and thick Which made it very hard to prick, He could not get through it with hacks and cuts Which made him cross in his heart and guts!	*Sir Eglamore pokes the dragon in the back with his sword, and looks angry. The dragon shakes her head, and laughs.*
INSTRUMENTAL VERSE	*Sir Eglamore chases the dragon around, and then the dragon chases Sir Eglamore around.*
4. But now as the knight with rage did burn He owed that dragon a right good turn, In at her mouth his sword he did send - The hilt appeared at the other end!	*Sir Eglamore stops, and grabs the dragon. He thrusts his sword down the dragon's throat. (Faked by passing the sword to the side of the dragon's face away from the audience. Leave sword on floor).*
5. The dragon like a coward began to fly Back to her den which was nearby, And there she laid her down and roared - The knight was cross for he'd lost his sword!	*The dragon flies back towards her den, stops outside it, gives a loud roar and drops down dead.*
INSTRUMENTAL VERSE	*The cast stands in a line facing the audience.*
6. Now God preserve our King and Queen That all round England may be seen As many knights - and many more As brave and good as Sir Eglamore!	*All sing out to the audience. Sir Eglamore raises his arms to show he's won. All cheer at end of song!*

COSTUMES

Sir Eglamore
Shape a helmet out of tin foil. Draw the foil up to a point at the top, and insert a feather or flag. The knight's tabard can be a rectangle of white material with a hole in the middle for a head, and with a large red cross on the front. A broomstick makes an excellent 'horse'.

Dragon
This dragon is portrayed by a triangular green cloak. Cut the edges in a zig-zag pattern to resemble the dragon's scales. (For more scales, cover the cloak with bits of triangular, green-coloured scraps.) Attach elastic cuffs to the corners for the wrists. Either use a mask, or paint the face green and frightening.

Hill
This can simply be a large brown or dark-green circle of material, about 6ft in diameter, and with a hole in the middle for the head. To symbolise a forest, the pupil playing the hill can hold a 'tree' or branch, with paper leaves attached.

Cave
To make the cave, two pupils hold up a grey, black or brown curtain, one at each end. The curtain should be approximately 1 × 1.5 metres. There should be a slit in the middle to allow the dragon to come out.

Other things to try

1. Look at, and discuss, paintings and statues that feature a dragon, especially those that also feature St George, such as Uccello's *St George and the Dragon*, hanging in the National Gallery. There is also a Tudor image of a dragon in the painting *The Field of the Cloth of Gold*, hanging in Hampton Court. It seems to be flying in the sky at the top left-hand corner of the painting. In fact, it is a firework for the celebrations. Use this picture to discuss not only dragons, but also the court of Henry VIII and his relations with other monarchs.

2. Story-telling. Pupils should sit in a circle and tell one another any dragon stories that they know. Pupils can also invent their own 'class story', each one adding a part of the tale. For example, the first pupil starts: *a fierce dragon lived in a cave on a hill*. A second pupil continues: *but he was lonely, and one day a knight came riding by*; then a third pupil: *when he saw the dragon he was scared, but the dragon invited him in for tea*. Try making up the stories in rhyme. If you end up with a good story, you could act it out using the Sir Eglamore costumes, and any others you wish to make.

TUDOR TOWN LIFE

When that I was a Little Tiny Boy

— CD Track 9 —

FOCUS ON:
Shakespeare

One of the focal points of a town was its theatre, and London had several. This song comes at the very end of Shakespeare's play Twelfth Night. *The singer (Feste, the Clown) is reflecting on the increasing harshness of life in the journey from childhood to old age. We do not know which melody was used by Shakespeare - the one used here is a popular Elizabethan dance tune.*

Listening and appraising

You can hear: SINGER, LUTE

There are five sung verses. Each one has two CHORUS phrases.

Things to talk about

1. Shakespeare's text has many layers of interpretation, but here are some suggestions as to the meaning of:

   a foolish thing was but a toy
   = a prank was just a bit of childish fun

   the rain it raineth every day
   = you just have to take what's coming

   a tosspot = a drunkard

2. Notice the slower speed in the last verse. *(for a reflective mood at the end of the play)*

3. The voice is accompanied by a lute. Discuss what 'accompanying' means. *(present and supporting - but not dominant)*

4. Pupils should notice the lute solo between each verse. Which part of the song does it play? *(it repeats the last phrase)*

5 Think about the rhythm: it has a gentle 'swinging' feel. Try counting two slow beats per bar as you listen.

6 Discuss the old-fashion word *raineth*.

7 Make sure pupils identify which phrases are the choruses (*With a hey...* and *For the rain...*). They should raise their hands each time they hear them.

Now - let's make Tudor music!

SINGERS:
First, learn the two choruses. Say the words in rhythm, then sing along with the track. Notice that the phrase *For the rain it raineth every day* starts on a high note - and the word *raineth* is sung across three note pitches: *rai-neth*.

Now have a go at the SOLO bits. Start singing after the two lute chords. Watch out for the phrase *With tosspots* (verse 4). The word *with* starts a little earlier than usual.

When everyone feels confident with the melody and words, divide up into two groups: SOLO singers and CHORUS singers. Individual pupils may even like to try a 'solo' on their own.

RECORDERS:
They only play in the choruses each time. This part uses a 'trill' - marked tr - a common feature of Tudor music. A trill means you play the printed note and the one above it, oscillating rapidly back and forth between them, in one breath. Start by playing the part without the trills, then play the part with the trills. Players should follow the words of the singers (printed underneath) to help stay in time.

TAMBORINES/SHAKERS/RAIN-MAKERS:
Play in the choruses only, making sure to stop crisply. Follow the words of the song (printed underneath) to help stay in time.

DRUMS/TABORS:
Play four even beats in both choruses. Follow the words of the song (printed underneath) to help stay in time.

TEACHER'S GUITAR PART (optional):
Teachers can reinforce the accompaniment by playing the guitar chords printed above the melody in the Pupil's Book. If you can provide this part, the song could also be performed without the CD.

Other things to try

1. Imagine performing this song on the stage at Shakespeare's theatre at the end of the play and discuss what it must have been like. Where do the instrumentalists sit? How far away are the audience? Are you alone on the stage? What do you do at the end of your performance - take a bow? Do the audience clap - or bang their feet and cheer?

2. Divide the class into two groups, each taking it in turns to perform this song to the other. Perhaps an Elizabethan audience might have joined in singing the choruses with the actor on stage?

3. Visit Shakespeare's Globe Theatre in Southwark, London. (Shakespeare's Globe, New Globe Walk, Southwark, London, SE1 9DT.)

Shakespeare's Globe on London's Bankside

HENRY VIII AND HIS SIX WIVES

Henry VIII's Song
'Pastime with Good Company'

— CD Tracks 10 and 11 —

FOCUS ON:
Singing difficult words to a steady drum beat

This is one of the Tudor period's most famous songs. It comes from the Court Song Book of Henry VIII, compiled some time before 1520, the contents of which would have been familiar to Henry and his courtiers. The King was a good musician - he could sing at sight and play a variety of instruments - and is said to have written this song. The text certainly reflects a younger, healthier and happier personality than that of the ill and troubled Henry of later years.

Listening and appraising

You can hear: SINGERS, DRUM, TREBLE REBEC, BASS REBEC, CURTAL, SHAWM

The piece is played four times:
    Verse 1: Singers and drum
    Instrumental verse
    Verse 2: Singers and instruments
    Instrumental verse

Things to talk about

1 Explain any difficult phrases, e.g. *Pastime with good company* = spending time with friends.

2 *Hunt, sing and dance* (in verse 1) shows what Henry and his friends enjoyed doing.

3 *So God be pleased* (in verse 1) shows the importance of religion to Henry.

4 What was Henry's frame of mind when he wrote this? *(happy and enjoying life)* Discuss the mood of the text in general.

5 Identify the instruments you can hear, their timbre, and what instrumental family they belong to. *(wind, stringed or percussion)* Notice how the drum plays the same rhythm throughout.

6 Which instrument plays the melody? *(treble rebec)*

7 Notice when the shawm joins in *(final verse)*. What does it play - is it the melody? *(it plays a decorative part above the melody)*

Now - let's make Tudor music!

Try for a lively and energetic performance - as cheerful as the words of the song.

SINGERS/RECORDERS:
Why not use the slower LEARNING TRACK (CD Track 11) first, to help pick up the melody. Then sing along with the main CD track, making sure the words are really clear.

DRUMS/TABORS:
Why not use the slower LEARNING TRACK (CD Track 11) first, to help pick up the drum rhythm. Clap it first *(slow - quick-quick)* then play it on your instruments with the main track.

Other things to try

Pupils can compose their own set of words to go with the two instrumental verses of this song in the following way. This song is about having fun with your friends. Identify the things Henry liked to do, and ask pupils what they like doing. Divide into seven groups. Each group decides between themselves ONE favourite activity and makes it into a short phrase, for example *riding my bicycle, eating lots of sweets* or *watching the telly*. The teacher (or a pupil) then starts to play the drum/tabor rhythm of the song *(slow - quick-quick)*, repeating it over and over. Each group finds a rhythmic way of chanting its own phrase in time with the drum/tabor's steady rhythm, like a rap. Each phrase should last two bars' length, e.g.

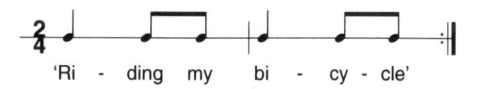

'Ri - ding my bi - cy - cle'

Now practise a 'call and response' exercise: each group in turn chants its own phrase, and the rest of the class echoes it immediately, copying the rhythm and words. These seven chants - each with its 'echo' - can now be fitted into the instrumental verses of the song *Pastime with Good Company*. You will have created a brand new version of this Tudor song by performing your new verses along with Henry's own!

HENRY VIII AND HIS SIX WIVES

Katherine of Aragon's Song
'Cross the Water'

— CD Tracks 12 and 13 —

FOCUS ON:
Spanish-style music

We often think of Henry VIII as having lots of short marriages, one after the other, but his first marriage, to the Spanish princess Katherine of Aragon, lasted nearly 20 years. This song comes from the Palace Song Book of the Court of Ferdinand and Isabella, in use around the time Katherine was growing up.

Listening and appraising

You can hear: SINGERS, SOPRANINO RECORDER, GUITAR, BASS VIOL, TAMBOURINE

There are two sections: the CHORUS and the VERSE. The piece runs like this:
Chorus Verse (solo singer) Chorus Verse (played on sopranino recorder) Chorus

Things to talk about

1 Imagine this song is about Katherine of Aragon coming to England from Spain as a young girl. Look at a map and decide which 'water' she might actually have crossed. *(the Channel, the Atlantic?)*

2 Pupils should raise their hands to indicate when:
- the CHORUS starts
- the recorder SOLO begins *(2nd verse)*
- the rhythm changes *('orchards today')*

3 What do you think gives this song a Spanish feel? *(tambourine shakes, guitar strumming)*

4 Notice that Katherine's name is pronounced in the Spanish way, *Katerina*.

Now - let's make Tudor music!

SINGERS (sing in choruses only*):
Why not use the slower LEARNING TRACK (CD Track 13) first, to help pick up the melody. Then sing along with the main CD track, coming in after the guitar strums. Use a strong, energetic voice and really feel the swinging rhythm. Watch out for the quick notes on the first two syllables of the word 'Kat-er'(ina). Don't forget the chorus is repeated each time.

RECORDERS/VIOLINS (play in choruses only):
This part is the same as for the singers. Why not use the slower LEARNING TRACK (CD Track 13) first, to help pick up the melody. Then play along with the main CD track. Feel the swinging rhythm and make sure that repeated notes are short - they should be 'tongued'. Don't forget the chorus is repeated each time.

CHIME BARS (play in choruses only):
You need notes C, D, F and A (in ascending order). Make sure the speed is correct - it will help to follow the singers' words printed below the notes. Don't forget the chorus is repeated each time.

TAMBOURINES (choruses only):
Why not use the slower LEARNING TRACK (CD Track 13), to help pick up the rhythms. First, practise doing individual shakes and taps, making sure they sound different from each other: the shakes should be even and vigorous; the taps should be short and crisp. Now look carefully at the written part and see how the shakes and taps fit in with the words of the chorus. Make sure the shakes keep going for the full four beats. Don't forget the chorus is repeated each time.

TEACHER'S GUITAR PART (optional):
If you play the guitar, you can help by playing the chords printed above the melody in the Pupil's Book. You could then try and perform this song without the CD track.

*After learning the chorus and listening to the CD track a few times, pupils may naturally pick up the solo verse as well. Why not choose a small group to sing (or play) along with the verse, contrasting with the thicker texture of the main group singing and playing the chorus.

The words are:
*I walked into the orchard today,
I walked into the orchard today,
There I plucked three fine red roses
For Lady Katerina.*

Other things to try

1. Look at pictures of Flamenco dancers with their tambourines, guitars and castanets. In a performance of this song, players could shake the tambourine up in the air and round their head, keeping the shake going all the time.

2. Traditional Spanish dancing uses foot-stamping as part of the steps. Try foot-stamping on the words *orch-ards to-day* - first one stamp, then two stamps per syllable.

3. Discuss what happened to Katherine of Aragon after Henry met Anne Boleyn.

Freemens Songs of 4. Voices.

The singing part.   TREBLE.

Martin said to his man fie man, fie, O Martin said to his man who's the foole now? Martin said to his man fill thou the cup and I the can, thou haft well drunken man, who's the foole now.

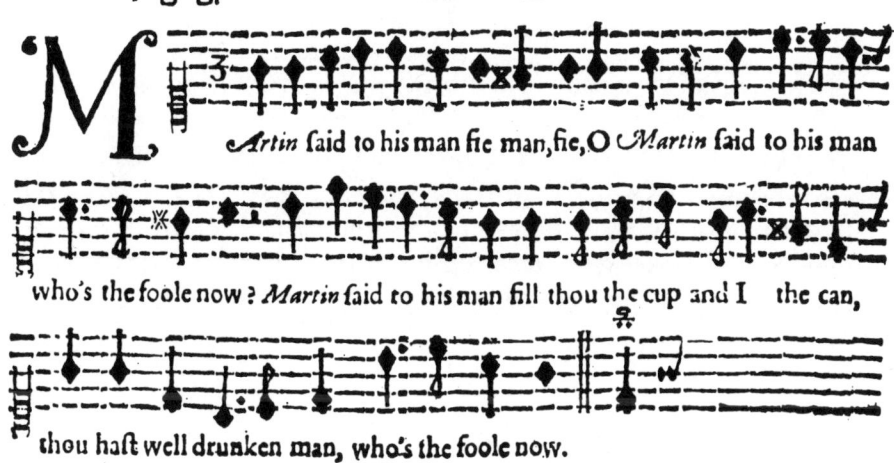

2 I see a sheepe shering corne,
   Fie man, fie:
I see a sheepe shearing corne,
   Who's the foole now?
I see a sheepe shearing corne,
And a couckold blow his horne,
   Thou haft well drunken man,
   Who's the foole now?

3 I see a man in the Moone,
   Fie man, fie:
I see a man in the Moone,
   Who's the foole now?
I see a man in the Moone,
Clowting of Saint *Peters* shoone,
   Thou haft well, &c.

4 I see a hare chase a hound,
   Fie man, fie:
I see a hare chase a hound,
   who's the foole now?
I see a hare chase a hound,
Twenty mile aboue the ground,
   Thou haft well drunken man,
   Who's the foole now?

5 I see a goose ring a hog,
   Fie man, fie:
I see a goose ring a hog,
   Who's the foole now?
I see a goose ring a hog,
And a snayle that did bite a dog,
   Thou haft well, &c.

Part of the original printed music for Martin said to his Man *(see page 14)*

HENRY VIII AND HIS SIX WIVES

Anne Boleyn's Song
'Greensleeves'

— CD Track 14 —

FOCUS ON:
Breath control and pitch awareness in singing

This song is probably the most famous of all Tudor love songs. We do not know who wrote it, but the harmonic sequence upon which it is based is found in a great many songs and tunes of the period. The text (not all of which is printed here) suggests that it was sung by a gentleman to his courtesan, green being the colour of vice in this period. Here, however, the song lends itself perfectly as an expression of the love that Henry felt for Anne Boleyn.

Listening and appraising

You can hear: SINGER, LUTES

There are three verses, each with a chorus.

Things to talk about

1 'Greensleeves' is the lady's nickname. How does the man feel about her and why is he complaining? List the gifts he has given her. What sort of modern equivalents might a rich man give a woman he loves?

2 Make sure everyone knows which bit is the chorus.

3 TEXTURE: What instruments accompany the voice? *(lutes)* How are they played? Use words to describe the sound.

4 PITCH: Which word has the highest note? *(Greensleeves)* Which word has the lowest note? *(de-light)* Why do you think the word 'Greensleeves' is always sung on the highest note? *(to add emotional force, pleading, show her importance, etc.)* Notice that the chorus melody starts high in pitch, and each phrase gradually descends in pitch. This adds to the impression of a 'sighing lover'.

Now – let's make Tudor music!

SINGERS:
Learn the CHORUS first. The first note is quite high in pitch – think of it in your head first, just before you start singing. Sing the song gently and reflectively, quietly enough to be able to hear the lute accompaniment on the track. The phrases are long – sitting up straight will increase lung capacity! Try taking breaths at the places marked √. You may like to try learning the VERSES as well. Notice the word *liked* in the last verse – it is sung on two syllables: *lik-ed*.

CHIME BARS:
You need notes D, E, G, B (in ascending order). Get your speed (tempo) from the two chords played on the lute at the very beginning. The music is the same for verse and chorus, so play along with both if you like.

Other things to try

The singer is trying to show his love by giving the lady fine presents. Pupils could make up their own song to someone they admire or love, perhaps a relation, friend, teacher, dog or cat.

On a xylophone (or on other tuned instruments) establish a steady, slow, repeating bass-note pattern (an *ostinato*). Use the notes E, D, C, B, in descending order, as follows:

    E E E E   D D D D   C C C C   B B B B

Chant the words of your poem to the regular beat of the bass pattern – or, if possible, make up a melody and *sing* the poem. It's best to use one line of poetry to each group of four repeated notes.

Don't forget the sentiment of your song or poem. It's all about love, so experiment with different ways of singing: gently and quietly, perhaps even whispering. For added expression you could also experiment by replacing the chime-bar bass pattern with singing the same notes gently to *la*.

HENRY VIII AND HIS SIX WIVES

Jane Seymour's Tune
'The Sick Tune'

— CD Tracks 15 and 16 —

FOCUS ON:
The effects of using different tempi and instruments
Inventing a text to an existing tune

The original title of this little piece, The Sick Tune, has inspired us to use it here to illustrate the fears and consequences of illness in Tudor times. Henry, when he married the young Jane Seymour, was already unhealthy and worried he would catch the deadly 'sweating sickness' (there was currently an epidemic). Medical intervention, being very limited, often made the patient worse rather than better. Jane herself died in childbirth from a fever, and her son, later Edward VI, died slowly and painfully at the age of 15, possibly from the arsenic that was administered to him as a medicine.

Listening and appraising

You can hear: CURTAL, SOPRANO CRUMHORN, LUTE, BASS VIOL

The piece is played three times:
- 1st time - melody on curtal
- 2nd time - melody (faster) on soprano crumhorn (fast)
- 3rd time - melody on curtal

Things to talk about

1 Identify the instruments that play the melody. How are they played? *(wind, strings, etc.)* Describe their timbre.

2 TEMPO (speed): The 2nd time through (led by soprano crumhorn) is twice as fast as the 1st and 3rd times.

3 PHRASES (marked ⌐⎺⎺⎺⎤): notice how these get longer as the piece progresses.

4 Can you hear/identify the two accompanying instruments which are playing throughout? *(lute and bass viol)*

5 The MOOD of the piece - does it change? Where?

Now - let's make Tudor music!

RECORDERS:
On the CD track, this is the part you can hear played by the curtal. Start after the two lute chords. Recorders play on the 1st and 3rd times through. More proficient players could also try playing in the fast bit (2nd time through).

CHIME BARS/VIOLINS/BASS XYLOPHONE:
You need notes D and E (in ascending order). Use the LEARNING TRACK (CD Track 16) to pick up the *slow - quick-quick* rhythm. Play all through if possible - even in the fast bit!

TEACHER'S GUITAR PART (optional):
Teachers who play the guitar can try the guitar chords printed over the recorder part in the Pupil's Book. With this part, you could play the piece without the CD track.

Other things to try

Make up your own song to *The Sick Tune*. The words don't have to be about feeling ill or miserable - but this may be a good starting theme.

Your song words should follow the natural shape of the music. Be aware of the phrases and note-patterns *within* the melody:

Phrases 1 and 2 have the same *note-pattern* - lyrics could reflect this by using similar words for both phrases. Phrase 3 is twice as long and can have more words; phrase 4 longer still:

1st line of music:

          1   2   3
I feel sick, very sick, lying here in my bed all day.

2nd line of music:

                   4
Tummy's aching, head is throbbing, hope I'll soon feel better.

HENRY VIII AND HIS SIX WIVES

Anne of Cleves' Dance
'The Dance of Cleves'

— CD Tracks 17 and 18 —

FOCUS ON:
Reading rhythm patterns

For political reasons, it was decided that England should be allied with Germany - and that Henry's fourth wife should be the Duke of Cleves' sister, Anne. This dance tune is from the town of Cleves. It's a Basse dance, an old version of the Pavan (see Queen Elizabeth's Almain page 66), and was known throughout the Low Countries and England.

Listening and appraising

You can hear: FLEMISH BAGPIPE, HURDYGURDY, DRUM

Things to talk about

1. How the bagpipe works. It plays both the MELODY and DRONE (a single long sustained note). Pick out and hum the pitch of the DRONE with the track. After a while you will run out of breath. Why doesn't this happen to the bagpiper? *(the air is stored in a bag)*

2. How the hurdygurdy works. It plays both the MELODY and DRONE. Listen to the *trompette* - the buzzing rhythmic effect.

3. The Kissing Music. After the dance has stopped you will hear an extra short phrase or two. This is known as 'Kissing Music' - a special moment when the couples thank each other for the dance. If you listen carefully you can hear Henry and Anne, saying 'thank you' over the Kissing Music!

4. Notice the rhythm of the INTRODUCTION before the dance starts: *long-short, short, short, short,* twice.

Now - let's make Tudor music!

ALL PLAYERS:
The LEARNING TRACK (CD Track 18) has a variety of percussion instruments and rhythms. Use instruments as near as possible to those suggested. Later you can experiment with your own rhythms and instruments - but start simply! Don't forget that the main track begins with an introduction. Pupils should start after this, once the dance rhythm gets going.

Other things to try

1 Look at paintings of people playing bagpipes - Dutch 17th-century pictures and anything by Breughel are good places to start.

2 The German/Flemish dance style was often considered rather heavy and clumsy with lots of foot-stamps and hand-claps. Working in pairs, pupils could try inventing a rhythmic sequence, part 'dance', part body-percussion, clapping each other's hands and stamping in time to the music. Each sequence should be memorised and repeated. Try a variety of different sequences, one after the other, without the track but keeping the pulse steady.

HENRY VIII AND HIS SIX WIVES

Catherine Howard's Song
'When I was a Maiden'

— CD Tracks 19 and 20 —

FOCUS ON:
A demanding recorder part
A consort of rebecs

Catherine Howard was young and much admired when she came to court, although her flirtatiousness led to her final undoing. This song (original title And I were a Maiden*) comes from the* Court Song Book of Henry VIII, *a volume published before 1520, containing many of the popular songs and tunes that were heard at the King's court.*

Listening and appraising

You can hear: SINGER and a consort of REBECS

The song opens with an instrumental verse, followed by three sung verses.

Things to talk about

1 Do you think Catherine Howard was a bit like the girl in the song?

2 How would you describe the MOOD of the song? *(gentle, simple, sweet? etc.)*

3 Any difficult words e.g. *amiss, courtiers*.

4 Notice how the second half of each verse is repeated.

5 TEXTURE: the singer is accompanied by five rebecs. What do they look like, how is the sound produced? *(bowed)*

6 TIMBRE: in this period a group of instruments of the same type, playing together, is called a consort. This song features a consort of rebecs, in different sizes. CD Track 34 *The Spanish Pavan* features a consort of *viols* - compare the sound of these two different types of bowed instruments by switching from track to track.

46

7 In this song, the rebecs ACCOMPANY the singer. What does this mean? *(they are present but not dominant)* They also have their own verse at the beginning.

8 The PITCH range of the melody is quite limited and it uses only six different notes. Pupils should raise their hands to indicate when they hear the *highest* note, and when they hear the *lowest* note. It will help to follow the notation in the Pupils' Book.

Now - let's make Tudor music!

SINGERS:
Come in after the instrumental verse. Hum along quietly at first, to get to know the melody. Look out for the *pitch* in bar 4 (e.g. the word *is* in verse 2). Sing gently and sweetly, and try taking a breath where marked √.

RECORDERS:
First use the slower LEARNING TRACK (CD Track 20). Start playing with the main track when the singers start. You can take a breath where the music is marked √.

CHIME BARS:
You need notes G, A, B, C (in ascending order). Make sure everyone understands the difference between the black notes *(crotchets)* worth one beat, and the white notes *(minims)* worth two beats. It will help to follow the singer's words (written underneath) as you play. You start playing when the singers begin.

Other things to try

Look at books on heraldry, and discuss the significance of personal and family crests. Royalty and aristocracy have always had their own motifs and emblems, often reflecting their owner's personality. As Queen, Catherine took the rose crowned - symbol of beauty, royalty and innocence - as her emblem. Pupils could draw Catherine's crest, or design crests or ceremonial flags for each other, reflecting surnames, characters and interests. These could be made into flags or banners to decorate the performing space when presenting the music and drama projects in this book.

HENRY VIII AND HIS SIX WIVES

A Sailor's Dance for Catherine Parr

— CD Tracks 21 and 22 —

FOCUS ON:
Improvising over an ostinato bass
Making musical choices

It was during his last marriage to Catherine Parr that Henry's famous flagship, the Mary Rose, unexpectedly sank before his eyes at Portsmouth harbour in 1545. Several musical instruments were found in the wreck when it was raised in 1982, including a simple wooden pipe - presumably brought aboard by one of the sailors.

Listening and appraising

You can hear: PIPE and TABOR

This piece uses as its framework a melody made up of three musical phrases played over an ostinato bass (a musical pattern that is repeated many times). First we hear the melody in its simplest form:

Phrase 1

Phrase 2

Phrase 3

Then we hear the player IMPROVISING more of these three-phrase melodies over the same repeating bass sequence. There are seven VARIATIONS, each one exploring a little musical idea.

Things to talk about

1 Try to spot when a new VARIATION starts. (indicate by raising hands)

2 Each pupil writes a vertical list of numbers from 1 to 8 on a sheet of paper, each

representing a melodic variation. After listening a few times they will be able to put a tick against the number of the improvisation they liked best or least. Are any especially popular? This exercise, as well as being fun, will help pupils to gain a sense of the phrase structure of the piece and prepare them to join in the next stage.

Now - let's make Tudor music!

This piece is all about improvising over a REPEATING BASS SEQUENCE. It offers pupils the chance to make their own *musical choices* within the framework set by the bass sequence. It therefore provides a valuable bridge between *playing* and *composing* since both elements are present. Have fun - and at the end discuss your results!

As a warm-up:
Everyone sits in a circle and claps the slow, regular pulse along with the track. Then, on a signal, clap in *double* time (i.e. twice as fast), then twice as fast again. Also, try clapping slowly, at half-speed. Now clap the same rhythm that the tabor on the track plays at the beginning: *Slow-slow-quick-quick-slow.*

Now - divide the class into three groups:

CHIME-BARS 1/BASS XYLOPHONE/CELLOS:
This group plays the **REPEATING BASS SEQUENCE**

The notes you need are: C, F, G (you can use high-C or low-C, or a mixture of both). First, why not use the slower LEARNING TRACK (CD Track 22) to help get the speed of the pulse. Start playing after the drum introduction on the track. Once pupils can play accurately the notes of the three-phrase bass sequence in their books, they can try inventing rhythms to make it more interesting. Get ideas for rhythms from what the pipe is playing and from the natural rhythms of words like *ca-ter-pil-lar, sau-sa-ges* or *rain-drops*.

CHIME-BARS 2/RECORDERS:
This group improvises a *melody*.
Pupils move from circle to circle in time with the bass sequence, selecting one note from each circle. Each time the sequence comes around again, they may choose a different set of notes. After a few goes through, some pupils may have begun to improvise a melody line which they like, and can memorise. They could play these to the rest of the class. N.B. Encourage pupils to *listen* as they play (rather than just following the circles by sight).

PERCUSSION:
Start after the drum introduction on the CD track, copying its rhythm. Then explore different effects like long and short beats, shakes, rhythms based on words, dynamic variations - even drop out for a few phrases if you feel like it. But don't get too carried away - always stay in time with the basic pulse.

TEACHER'S GUITAR PART (optional):
Teachers who play the guitar can reinforce the repeating bass sequence by playing the chords C - F - G - C repeatedly.

Other things to try

1. A simple wooden three-hole pipe, which could be played with just the left hand, was often teamed up with a tabor, which the player beat with his other hand. Think about the difficulties - and advantages - of playing *two* instruments at the same time. Recorder players could try holding their instrument in the left hand only and playing three notes: B, A, G. Put a drum on a nearby table and, holding a drum stick in the right hand, beat in time to the recorder, then try contrasting rhythms. Non-recorder players could experiment by holding a drum stick in each hand and tapping two drums (placed one either side) at the same time, in different rhythms. This is the kind of thing that pop and rock drummers do on a drum kit.

2. Discuss how the discovery of ancient musical instruments, like those on the *Mary Rose*, can help us know what instruments looked like. All the instruments heard on the CD are *replicas*, copied from paintings, carvings or manuscripts of the period. Good examples are found in 16th- and 17th-century Dutch paintings or in stone carvings like those in Beverley Minster, Yorkshire.

3. Visit Portsmouth and see the *Mary Rose*, preserved by the Mary Rose Trust. (Details from The Mary Rose Trust, College Road, H.M. Naval Base, Portsmouth PO1 3LX.)

The main gallery for viewing the Mary Rose

TUDOR SPORTS AND PASTIMES

Tomorrow the Fox will come to Town

— CD Tracks 23 and 24 —

FOCUS ON:
Compound time

This catchy call-to-the-hunt describes the harm a fox could do in farmyards and small holdings up and down the country. It comes from a collection of popular songs and rounds published by Thomas Ravenscroft - a composer better known for writing hymns!

Listening and appraising

You can hear: FOUR SINGERS, REBEC, CITTERN, CURTAL

There are four sung verses and two instrumental verses.

Things to talk about

1 How many verses can you hear? How many are sung and how many are for instruments only? Each verse names a different animal in danger from the fox. *(hen, lamb, duck)*

2 Each verse ends with a chorus that starts: *I must desire...* Pupils should raise hands to indicate when they hear the chorus start.

3 The *Whoop, whoop!* is a vocal imitation of the sound of a hunting horn. If you listen carefully you can hear a hunting horn on the track just before the song starts.

4 *Oh keep you all well there!* means 'guard your animals well'.

5 What instrument plays the lead part in the two instrumental verses? *(rebec)*

6 Identify the lowest instrument *(curtal)* and discuss how the cittern's 'jangly sound' might derive from its metal strings.

52

7 The song has a strong four-square pulse - the strong beats are underlined:

1 (2 · 3)	**2** (2- 3)	**3** (2- 3)	**4** (2-3)
'To | **mo**rrow the	**fox** will	**come** to	**town**...'

Pupils should tap this pulse quietly along with the track, counting up to four as they listen. Now, in this song, each of these strong beats can be also divided into three quick beats. Pupils should count the quick '1-2-3s' out loud as they continue to tap the four strong pulses. This is called *compound time* and it helps to give this piece its bouncy, dance-like feel.

Now - let's make Tudor music!

SINGERS:
First, why not learn the melody with the LEARNING TRACK (CD Track 24). Now sing along with the main track, starting after the count of four. Try and make the *whoops* bouncy and crisp. You could also try dividing the class into smaller groups who sing a verse each, while everyone else joins in the choruses.

CHIME-BAR DRONE PLAYERS:
You need notes D, G, A (in ascending order). Play your beats steadily, in time with the pulse of the song, starting after the count of four.

VIOLINS/CELLOS:
Pluck or bow the part, starting after four.

Other things to try

A listening and movement exercise. One pupil is the fox, three pupils play instruments, and the rest are hens, lambs or ducks. The farm animals walk around the 'farmyard', whispering *Tomorrow the fox will come to town* in the rhythm of the song. Periodically, the instrumentalists make sounds that the animals obey (anyone not obeying is out): tambourines - ducks freeze; triangles - lambs bleat; drums - hens lie down. Instruments play again to restart their group. Then the fox, shouting *Whoop, whoop!* runs into the centre. Each creature makes its own noise, and the fox must catch (touch) one of each kind of animal.

TUDOR SPORTS AND PASTIMES

Robin Hood and the Poacher

— CD Track 25 —

FOCUS ON:
A story in a song
Improvising percussion

This is one of many songs about Robin Hood that survive both in the written and the aural tradition. A favourite springtime activity at the Tudor court was the 'May Games and Disguisings' - a yearly ritual dating back to pagan times. As part of these festivities the King and Queen and their courtiers would dress up in the rough clothes of foresters and act out stories of Robin Hood and his gang of outlaws. A chronicle of the time describes the activities thus:

The King and Queen, accompanied by many Lords and Ladies, rode out to take the open air. As they passed by the way, they espied a company of tall yeomen, clothed all in green with green hoods and bows and arrows, to the number of two hundred. Then one of them, who called himself Robin Hood, came to the King, desiring him to see his men shoot, which much pleased the King and Queen. All these archers were of the King's Guard and had thus apparelled themselves to amuse the Royal party. Then Robin Hood desired the King and Queen to come to his greenwood and see how the outlaws live. There they found an arbour made of boughs and covered with flowers and sweet herbs which the King much praised. Then the King and Queen sat down and were served with an outlaw's breakfast of venison and wine by Robin and his men, to their great contentment.

Listening and appraising

You can hear: SINGERS, DRUM, HARP, REBEC, HURDYGURDY, BAGPIPE, TABOR

There are eight sung verses plus one instrumental verse at the end. The instruments enter one at a time as follows:

Verse 1 - singer and bass rebec
Verse 2 - add drum
Verse 3 - add tabor
Verse 4 - add harp
Verse 5 - add hurdygurdy (drone)
Verse 6 - add treble rebec
Verse 7 - add hurdygurdy (tune)
Verse 8 - add bagpipe
Instrumental Verse - add hurdygurdy trompette

Things to talk about

1 This ballad tells a story. What happens? What is Arthur doing in the forest? *(poaching deer)*

2 What is the job of the *keeper of the forest* in verse 3? What is a poacher?

3 What do the chorus singers do? *(they repeat the last line of each verse, adding the word 'Aye')* What does 'Aye' mean? *(yes).*

4 What do you notice about the TEXTURE of the song? *(it builds up verse by verse)*

5 Identify the instruments one by one as they enter.

6 Sometimes the hurdygurdy plays a DRONE (the *same* one or two notes played continuously), and sometimes it plays the MELODY line. Can you hear the difference?

7 Notice the hurdygurdy *trompette* in the last verse.

8 The MOOD: discuss how the regular drum and tabor beats add excitement and danger.

9 The notes of the MELODY are in 'threes'. To get the feel of this, tap along with the drum in verse 2, fitting a count of three on every beat.

Now – let's make Tudor music!

SINGERS:
Sing strongly with bravado. Join in the choruses first. Then try singing along with the verses too, starting after the introductory rebec drone. Watch out for the last word in the verse (just before the chorus) – it is always sung on *two* notes. As you get to know the song, vary the performance by dividing into two groups: Verse singers and Chorus singers. You could also

enhance the drama of the story by dividing into
four groups, each singing the appropriate parts:

1. Narrator   - verses 1, 6, 7, 8;
2. Robin Hood   - verses 2, 3, 5;
3. Arthur   - verse 4;
4. Choruses   - sung by all

Sit in a circle so that everyone can see each other - really try to bring the story to life with your eyes and voice.

MIXED PERCUSSION:
Build up the texture by adding a variety of different percussion instruments, one verse at a time. They should all play a simple *one-beat-per-bar* which builds up the tension. Then in verses 6, 7 and 8 (the fight), try adding extra beats, varying the rhythms to make it more exciting. Other effects that would work well in these verses are tambourine shakes and 'stick noises' such as claves, wood blocks and guiras.

Other things to try

Try acting out the song, or create a piece of music, based on a Robin Hood story, by building up a sound texture, layer by layer, adding one new instrumental group at a time.

Divide the class into seven groups of like instruments, for example: triangles, glockenspiels, recorders, drums, tambourines, shakers, bells. Each group represents one of the various items of booty stolen by Robin Hood from the rich to give to the poor. The class can decide what each instrument represents, such as triangle for *diamonds*, drum for a *strong horse*, shakers for *silver and gold*, bells for *silver spoons* etc. Pupils invent rhythms to play which follow the natural rhythm of the names.

Everyone sits in a circle, the members of each instrumental group sitting together. One pupil in the middle is the 'conductor' who starts to tell the story: *On Monday, Robin Hood came out of the forest and stole... diamonds!* The conductor points to the group representing diamonds, who begin a rhythm based on the word. They continue playing while the conductor continues: *On Tuesday, Robin Hood came out of the forest and stole ... silver and gold!* The conductor points to the respective group, who play their rhythm based on the words silver and gold.

Keep going through all the days of the week, leaving the louder instruments until later to build up the general volume gradually. Robin Hood's booty is often precious and beautiful. Make sure pupils reflect this in the way they play. Gentle playing will also help them hear the words of the story.

Some images of archers to share with the class

TUDOR SPORTS AND PASTIMES

Three Blind Mice
Singing with friends

— CD Tracks 26 and 27 —

FOCUS ON:
Singing a round
The oral tradition

Singing simple rounds and part-songs was a popular and sociable pastime in Tudor times, singing at sight being an important social skill. This song, one of many popular English songs, passed down the generations by ear. You will probably know it as a nursery rhyme, although, since it has naturally evolved and changed over the centuries, this early version is a little different.

Listening and appraising

You can hear: THREE SINGERS

This is a ROUND in three parts - the singers all sing the same music in a repeating harmonic pattern, but starting at different times. Each singer sings the song three times through and then drops out.

Things to talk about

1 How is this version different from the nursery rhyme we know today? *(it is in the minor key and is in a marching rhythm, simple duple, rather than a swinging rhythm, compound duple)*

2 Talk about how songs are passed down the centuries, often from mother to child. Is this still happening today? Think of some songs you know such as *Happy Birthday*, and *Twinkle Twinkle Little Star*. Do you remember where and when you first heard them? Did anyone teach them to you? These could be examples of an aural tradition, still thriving. Does everyone know the same version? Think of the game Chinese Whispers and how things change with time.

3 How does a ROUND work? Why do you think it is sometimes called a CATCH? (*the parts seem to be chasing each other*)

4 What is *tripe*? (*part of an ox's stomach*)

5 Pupils should raise their hands as they hear each singer start.

6 Look at the printed music in the Pupil's Book. Find note patterns that repeat. (*bars 1 and 2 are the same as bars 3 and 4; bar 5 is the same as bar 7*) Find words that repeat.

Now - let's make Tudor music!

SINGERS:

1 First, why not pick up the tune from the LEARNING TRACK (CD Track 27) which is slower. Speak the words in rhythm first, then sing along with the track. Watch out for the very first note - the song is in the MINOR key and the first note is therefore a little *flatter* (lower) than you might be expecting. Make sure to get the short notes of *merry old wife* crisp and clear.

N.B. Notice that just before they stop, the singers on the LEARNING TRACK repeat the first phrase once more, finally stopping on the word *mice*. In your performance, make sure each group does this too - but only the very last time, before they drop out.

2 When everyone has sung the song together, divide into TWO groups. Group 1 starts and, as they begin the 2nd phrase, Group 2 joins them, starting from the beginning.

3 Now, divide into THREE groups. Each group starts from the beginning as the previous group begins the 2nd phrase. Sing the song round and round as many times as you like. On a signal, the groups drop out, one at a time, in the same order as they started, not forgetting to repeat the first phrase one more time before they stop.

If your class has some bold singers, you could try a performance with just one singer per part.

Other things to try

1 You may know some other rounds like *London's Burning*, *Frère Jacques* or *White Sand and Grey Sand* (the latter is based on a street cry, see page 18). Try singing them and discuss what are the special characteristics needed to make a round work - usually three or four short repetitive phrases, each one starting a little higher, within the same background harmonic sequence.

2 Try a game of Chinese Whispers, based on the rhythm and words of *Three Blind Mice* or invent your own!

Part of the original printed music for Three Blind Mice

QUEEN ELIZABETH I

Eliza is the Fairest Queen

— CD Tracks 28 and 29 —

FOCUS ON:
Recreating a Tudor masque
Miming to a story

This song, in praise of Queen Elizabeth I, was originally performed in 1591 as part of an entertainment given by the Earl of Hertford in her honour. It was written by the composer Edward Johnson and was sung by performers dressed as a Fairy Queen and her maids who also 'danced about the garden'. It was said that this spectacle so delighted Her Majesty that she 'desired to hear it twice o'er'! The text reflects the popular portrayal of Elizabeth as the chaste Queen of the Fairies, and also her role as a revered political figure 'both bringing peace and stopping wars'.

Listening and appraising

You can hear: SINGER, VIRGINALS, TREBLE VIOL, BASS VIOL

The whole piece is played twice:
    1st time - instruments only
    2nd time - sung

Things to talk about

1. The virginals, how it works and how it is different from a piano (see page 87). Find words to describe its timbre.

2. Talk about what a viol looks like and how it is played. (Also see *The Spanish Pavan*, page 82, for a *viol consort*.)

3. What is the role of the bass viol in this piece? *(to reinforce the bass notes of the virginals and match the smoother tone of the vocal line against the 'short and spiky' staccato tone of the virginals)*

4. The treble viol, and how it plays the same tune as the singer. *(it plays the melody first time round)*

5 *Eliza* is the shortened form of the name Elizabeth. Notice how the repetition of the word *Eliza* gives the effect of an almost reverential chant. How many times is it sung? Notice that it almost always has the same musical rhythm.

6 The portrayal of Elizabeth as a *Fairy Queen*, in her *bower* and walking *upon the green*. *(pastoral images)*

7 The mention of her political power. *(both bringing peace, and stopping wars)*.

8 You may notice the rhythm of this song contains unusual stresses and cross-rhythms. This is typical of songs of the period.

Now - let's make Tudor music!

SINGERS:

Sing only on the second time through. Learn when to start by listening to the CD track: at the end of the first time through, the virginals plays two short chords just before you enter. Hum or sing quietly with the track while you learn the song. Notice that in the printed music there are beats where you have to stay quiet for a moment (𝄽 = a rest, a natural place to take a breath). Sing prettily, stressing the word *Eliza* whenever it comes.

RECORDERS:

Play both times through. There is a LEARNING TRACK (CD Track 29) to help the recorders master this part. On this track you start after the count of '1, 2, 3'. The notes marked ♩ should be played short (*staccato*). Take breaths where marked √, and in any natural gaps.

After practising with the LEARNING TRACK, play along with the main track. This time, start playing after you hear two slow chords on the virginals.

Making a performance

This piece can be acted out to create a scene like the Fairies' dance performed before Queen Elizabeth. You may like to invent your own ideas for movement, but here are our suggestions.

Divide the class into singers, recorder players, dancers (8-10 pupils) and actors (3 pupils take the parts of Queen Elizabeth, The Earl of Hertford, and the composer himself, Edward Johnson).

Singers and recorders sit where indicated, and begin playing. During the first instrumental verse the three actors lead in a procession of fairy dancers. They all reach their positions in good time, facing into the circle. Then, as the song begins, the dancers move as follows.

WORDS OF THE SONG	DANCERS' STAGE DIRECTIONS
'Eliza, Eliza'	*Gesture with head and outstretched arms towards the Queen, then drop down quickly.*
'Eliza is the fairest Queen, that ever trod upon the green'	*Stand up, hold hands, facing into circle. Step lightly to centre of circle, then all turn to face the Queen.*
'Eliza, Eliza'	*Gesture with head and outstretched arms towards the Queen as before.*
'Eliza's eyes are blessed stars'	*Facing Queen, make large arc with arms, looking up at the 'stars'.*
'Both bringing peace'	*Still facing Queen, kneel on one knee, arms and heads lowered.*
'And stopping wars'	*Still kneeling, hands across faces as if shielding them.*
'O blessed be each day and hour'	*Stand and walk to final tableau position.*
'Where sweet Eliza builds her bower'	*Hold final tableau. (Plan this beforehand: it should be a 'classical' arrangement, arms and bodies somewhat intertwined, some kneeling, some standing - all facing towards the Queen. Have a look at some pastoral pictures of nymphs. Make use of angles of heads and arms.)*
	As the music finishes, the royal party clap and congratulate everyone. Perhaps Queen Elizabeth could even demand a repeat performance!

Other things to try

1. Look at pictures of Queen Elizabeth and notice how she is portrayed in art of the period, even when old and ugly. (She was already 58 years old when this song was written.)

2. Discuss what sort of costume 'fairy dancers' might wear.

QUEEN ELIZABETH I

Queen Elizabeth's Almain

— CD Track 30 —

FOCUS ON:
Learning to dance the Almain

The Almain was one of the most popular dances at the Tudor court, its simple steps allowing time for the dancers to chat to each other. It was also known as The Peacock Dance because it gave people a chance to be seen and admired as they moved around the dance floor. (The little 'hop' enabled the men to show off the brightly coloured rosettes on their shoes!) Schools with more advanced instrumentalists may like to try playing the dance. You will find the music printed at the end of this section, with suggestions for instrumentation.

The music used here is called the *Mohrentanz* (literally 'The Moors Dance') and it comes from a collection by the Flemish composer Tylman Susato. It is heard on a variety of instruments all played over a bass viol and drum beat. First on four loud woodwind instruments (two rauschpfeifes and two curtals); then on a consort of four recorders; then on rebecs and crumhorns; and finally the loud wind instruments again.

The music has been recorded with the dance steps 'called' over it. However, for performance purposes you can eliminate the voice by turning down the RIGHT HAND speaker on your CD player. (Don't forget to turn it back up again before going on to the next piece!)

The Basic Movements

An Almain is basically made up of rhythmic 'walking steps':

The 'Single'
This occupies TWO counts
Starting with the L foot:
    1 Step forward with the L foot
    2 Draw the R foot up to join it

Starting with the R foot:
    1 Step forward with the R foot
    2 Draw the L foot up to join it

The 'Double'
This occupies FOUR counts:
    1 Step forward with the L foot
    2 Step forward on to the R foot
    3 Step forward on to the L foot
    4 Draw the R foot up to join it
(the next 'Double' would start on the R foot, and so on)

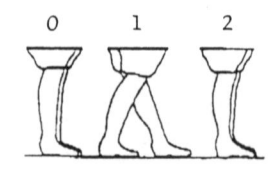

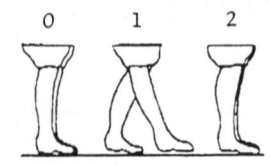

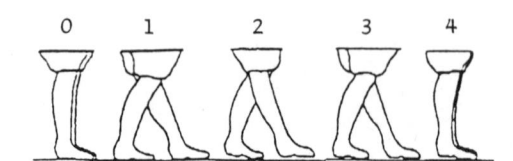

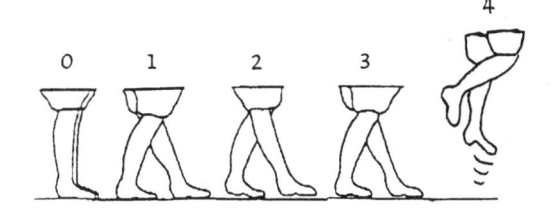

The 'Double with Hop'
This is the same as the 'Double', but instead of drawing the foot up at the end, you hop.
1. Step forward with the L foot
2. Step forward on to the R foot
3. Step forward on to the L foot
4. Hop on the L foot

Practise doing all the different kinds of steps, starting on alternate feet. Try eight of each in a row.

1 THE REVERENCE (bow/curtsey)

This is a Tudor version of a formal handshake, used on meeting someone or taking leave of them. It was always used when inviting someone to dance. Always look at the person to whom you are reverencing.

The Bow (gentlemen)
1. Keep the R foot firmly on the floor and the R knee straight.
2. Draw the L foot straight back. Sit back on L foot, bending the knee, thus bowing to your lady.
3. If you are wearing a hat, remove it with your hand as you bend lower (this can be mimed). As you finish your bow, straighten up again and put your hat back on.

The Curtsey (ladies)
1. Stand with heels together, toes a little turned out.
2. Bend both knees gently, keeping the body straight. Lower your eyes for a moment.
3. Arise gently.

2 PROMENADING AROUND THE ROOM

Couples hold hands and line up behind each other in a large circle.

1st 'Double' - L, R, L, hop on left foot

2nd 'Double' - R, L, R, hop on right foot

3rd 'Double' - L, R, L, hop on left foot

4th 'Double' - R, L, R, no hop this time. Instead, partners take both hands and face one another.

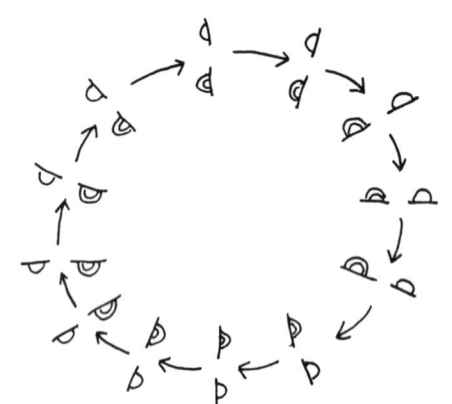

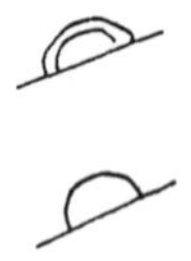

◠ = girl

◡ = boy

Couples walk round in a circle holding hands, with the girls on the inside.

3 CIRCLING IN COUPLES

Couples face each other holding both hands, first clockwise, then anticlockwise.

Clockwise: single, single, double
 ('step, together,
  step, together,
  step, step, step, together')

Anticlockwise: single, single, double*
 ('step, together,
  step, together,
  step, step, step, together')*

*On the final step of the last 'double', couples drop hands and get back in 'facing forward' position to *Promenade* again in a large circle round the room.

Continue alternatively promenading and circling for as long as you like - or until the music runs out! At the end of the dance, couples should *Reverence* to each other before leaving the dance floor.

The Queen's Almain
(Mohrentanz)

Suggestions for instrumentation:

    Line 1 can be played on descant recorder, violin, flute or oboe.

    Lines 2 and 3 can be played on all the above plus treble recorder and trumpet (transpose up a tone).

    Line 4 can be played by cellos or other bass instruments.

QUEEN ELIZABETH I

Long Live Fair Oriana

— CD Track 31 —

FOCUS ON:
Listening to a madrigal

Queen Elizabeth was much loved and respected, and many painters portrayed her in an almost superhuman image. She was known as The Fairie Queen and, in this piece, compared to Oriana - a brilliant star constellation portraying a mighty hunter. This musical excerpt is from a collection of madrigals - a style of part-song using many voices - known as The Triumphs of Oriana. It was compiled in Elizabeth's honour by court composer Thomas Morley.

Listening and appraising

You can hear: SIX SINGERS, all repeating the phrase *Long live fair Oriana*.

Things to talk about

1 The voices start one after another in rapid succession, sometimes at a low pitch and sometimes at the same pitch, like an echo. How many 'entries' of the same words can you count?

2 Notice how the Bass part sings *Long live fair Oriana* very slowly on long held notes.

3 After all the elaborate part-singing is over, the piece finishes with a single held chord. Compare this to how *Three Blind Mice* (CD Track 26) ends, each voice stopping one at a time.

4 Ask pupils to try to recreate the note pitches of the last chord, by singing immediately after the song has finished. They can choose any note they heard in the chord, singing on the vowel *ah*. The notes that actually make

up the last chord of the madrigal are G, B and D. Did everyone choose one of those? (Check which notes they sang with chime bars or keyboard.) Discuss the results. You may find most people naturally choose the note G. This is because G is the 'key note' of the piece. This exercise demonstrates that all chords are made up of at least THREE notes (a *triad*).

Other things to try

1 Queen Elizabeth was given special names by those who admired her - *Oriana, The Fairie Queen, Gloriana* and *Eliza*. If the class were to give each other nicknames, what would they be and why?

2 There are many madrigal recordings on the market which the class would enjoy listening to. Look especially for anything by Thomas Morley or Thomas Weelkes - both composers from this period.

QUEEN ELIZABETH I

The Death of Queen Elizabeth

— CD Track 32 —

FOCUS ON:
Music to create a dramatic atmosphere

This piece is commonly known as the 'Deathbed Pavan' because its composer, John Bull, one of the most important musicians of the Chapel Royal, wrote it in tribute to Queen Elizabeth after her death. Here it has been linked with an eyewitness account of the Queen's last days, written by her cousin, Robert Carey.

Listening and appraising

You can hear: VIRGINALS

Since the piece is quite long it may not be necessary to play it in its entirety at this stage.

Things to talk about

1 Identify the instrument. How is the sound produced?

2 Trills (also see *When that I was a Little Tiny Boy*, page 30). The performer plays the printed note and the one above it, oscillating rapidly back and forth between them. In this piece, trills are used to prolong notes on an instrument, such as the virginals, that cannot produce a sustained tone.

Joining in

Pupils can create a presenation by reading the following text as the music is played. It should exactly fit the length of the music. However, where appropriate, feel free to shorten some of the longer passages - you can always fade out any extra music at the end.

Choose 12 READERS
They could stand in a line facing the audience and project their voices slowly and clearly. However, if they have to shout to be heard, turn the CD volume down!

Start the CD track. Let it run for about 15 seconds to establish the mood before READER 1 starts. Try to pace the reading to fit with the music - you may need to experiment a few times.

The Death of QUEEN ELIZABETH I

Music starts (let it run for about 15 seconds)

READER 1	The Queen was not well. She was now 69 years old, had caught a bad cold and was feeling very miserable. Some people thought she had lost the will to live.
READER 2	She had to use a stick when she climbed the steep stairs in her palace and even needed help to get off her horse. Her grand clothes now felt uncomfortable and heavy. Her fingers had swollen up, and her special coronation ring had become so tight that it had to be filed off.
READER 3	She would not take the medicines the doctors gave her. She grew worse and worse. When the Earl of Nottingham came to see her, she said:

READER 4
(as Queen Elizabeth):
> 'I feel as if I have a huge, heavy chain of iron tied around my neck - I no longer feel well.'

READER 3	Another friend tried to cheer her up with a funny poem he had written, but she only said:

READER 4
(as Queen Elizabeth):
'When you feel death coming near, these things are not amusing any more.'

READER 5 She had a bad fever. But she refused to go to bed and instead sat on a pile of cushions on the floor.

READER 4
(as Queen Elizabeth):
'Oh - I feel so thirsty - I feel as if I have a great heat in my stomach.'

READER 5 'Madam, you *must* go to bed.'

READER 4
(as Queen Elizabeth):
'Little man, little man - never use the word *must* to a Queen!'

READER 6 For four days the Queen sat on her cushions in her private chamber, eating nothing, saying nothing and staring at the ground. On the third day she put one of her fingers in her mouth and, after that day, she hardly took it out again. She just sat curled up like a baby, staring at the floor.

READER 7 At last she grew so weak that the doctors carried her to bed, where an abscess burst in her throat.

READER 4
(as Queen Elizabeth):
(in a weak voice) 'I feel a little better. Give me some soup to drink.'

READER 7 But soon she grew worse again. She ate nothing more and just lay on her side without speaking or looking at anyone.

READER 8 Her councillors and nobles gathered round her bed to ask if she agreed that her cousin James, from Scotland, should be the next King.

READER 4
(as Queen Elizabeth):

> She could not speak, but made a sign with her hand to show that she agreed. *(reader makes a sign)*

READER 9   In the evening, the Archbishop of Canterbury came in to say prayers. He knelt beside the bed but after half-an-hour his knees started to feel very sore. But the Queen made a sign with her hand, telling him he must go on praying. He went on for another half-an-hour - but again the Queen made a sign that he must not stop. Every time he told her how lovely it was in heaven she squeezed his hand - as if she knew she was going to be there soon herself.

READER 10   Finally the Queen became unconscious. She died in the early hours of the morning. The women around her bed began weeping.

READER 11   Robert Carey, the Queen's cousin, crept quickly and quietly out of the palace grounds. He mounted his best horse and galloped off as fast as he could, northwards to Scotland.

READER 12   At last, after an exhausting ride of 400 miles, Robert rode his panting and exhausted horse into the courtyard of James's Palace. Covered in mud and bruises, he was the very first person to tell James that he was now King of England as well as Scotland.

ALL   'Long live the King!'

(Music ends)

SIR FRANCIS DRAKE AND THE ARMADA

The Invincible Armada

— CD Track 33 —

FOCUS ON:
Story-telling and sound effects
Constructing your own stringed instrument

This song is a broadside ballad. These were popular songs printed on broadsheets and sold by pedlars in streets, markets and taverns up and down the country. Rather like newspapers, broadside ballads told of everything from a local hanging or remedy for the plague to political propaganda - in this case, the story of Sir Francis Drake and the Armada. Written in rhyme, these ballads were often sung to popular tunes of the day. The tune was known as Eighty-eight - a reference to 1588, the year the Armada took place.

Listening and appraising

You can hear: SINGER, SOPRANINO RECORDER, BUM FIDDLE

There are SIX sung verses.

Things to talk about

1. Broadside ballads like this one were an early form of newspaper. Do you think this tells the story of the Armada properly? How does it compare with TV and newspaper stories today? Imagine someone standing on a street corner and singing the news like this - would people listen nowadays? Or imagine a TV newsreader singing the news instead of reading it!

2. Listen to the low rhythmic instrument - what is it and how is it played?
   (a bum fiddle, played with a bow)
   N.B. Notes on making a bum fiddle are at the end of this section.

3 MOOD: the use of sopranino recorder and the steady beat of the bum fiddle help to create a mood of tension and excitement - and a battle-like feel, reminiscent of a military fife and drum.

4 Check that pupils understand any difficult words or phrases, e.g. *years of late, bravado, vassals.*

5 Note similar patterns: bars 1 and 2, and bars 4 and 5 have the same notes (taking bar 1 as the first *full* bar). Notice that this pattern is reminiscent of a military fanfare, matching the triumphant mood of the piece.

6 Note the number of beats before the singer starts *(four)*, and the number of beats between the verses *(two)*.

Now - let's make Tudor music!

SINGERS/RECORDERS 1:
Speak the words first in rhythm along with the track, all through the song. Then sing.

RECORDERS 2:
This is an easier part. Follow the words underneath to get the speed.

DRUM/BUM FIDDLE:
Play one beat per bar. Pick up the rhythm from the bum fiddle on the track and keep steady.

PERCUSSION - 'Battle Effects' (verses 5 and 6 only):
This is an opportunity for some creative musical sound effects of battle.

One group of percussion players plays a short rhythm pattern and the other group copies the same pattern, like an echo. Divide percussion players into pairs - two drummers, two tambourine players, two wood block players etc. Within each pair, one pupil represents the English, and the other the Spanish. The 'English' players lead - playing a two-bar pattern *loudly*; and then the 'Spanish' follow - copying the same pattern, but *quietly*.

It's better not to plan any rhythms in advance - let pupils improvise and copy. Decide which rhythms worked best and use them in your performance. You can use a mixture of any available percussion.

Other things to try

1 In a performance of this piece, try preceding it with a street ballad-singer or town-crier announcing he has some news, as in the following reading:

    Hear ye! I do bring great news this day from the South of England where My Lord Sir Francis Drake (the Queen's favourite) has won a miraculous victory against the Spanish! Hear ye! Hear ye! I bring good news!

    (all cheer as song starts)

2 Make up a song, or think of one you already know, that tells a story - perhaps even a true story (for example a Christmas carol). How about pop songs - do they ever tell a story?

BUM FIDDLE:
This is an instrument you can make yourself. In spite of its comical name, a bum fiddle was a real instrument in the 16th, 17th and 18th centuries. It was traditionally made out of an inflated pig's bladder but nowadays can be made simply as follows:

What you need:

- An inflated round balloon
- A stick - a metre length of 12mm dowling
- One-and-a-half metres of thick fishing wire
- A flexible plastic 30cm ruler
- Plenty of sticky tape
- A piece of string

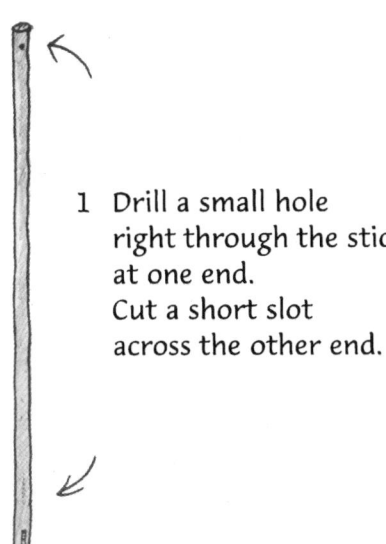

1 Drill a small hole right through the stick at one end. Cut a short slot across the other end.

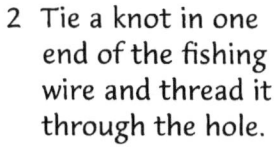

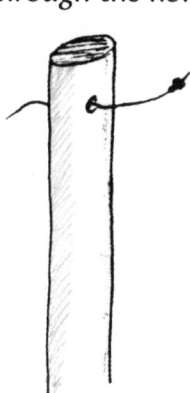

2 Tie a knot in one end of the fishing wire and thread it through the hole.

3 Tie a knot in the other end and thread through slot at other end.

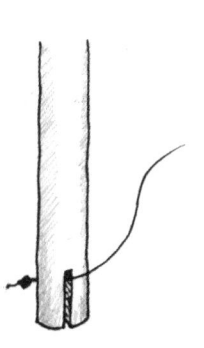

4 The fishing wire should be just a little longer than the stick.

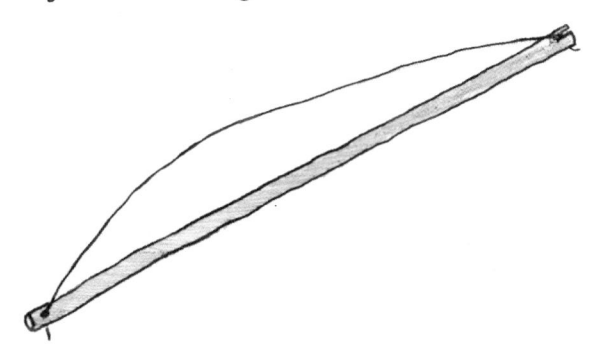

5 Inflate the balloon and tie a knot in the end.

6 Squeeze the inflated balloon between the stick and string - about 1/3 of the way down the stick.

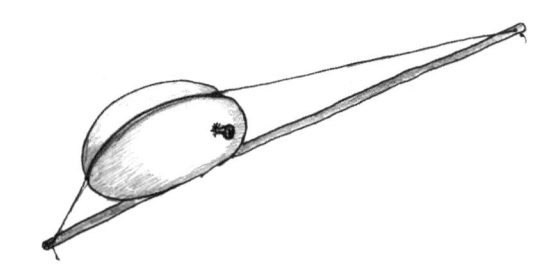

7 The string should now be tight enough to make a musical note when plucked. You can experiment by blowing up the balloon larger or smaller to get the pitch you want. Usually, the larger the balloon the tighter the string, and better the quality of the resulting note.

8 To make a bow, bend the plastic ruler as far as possible (without snapping it!). Hold it in that 'bowing' position with a length of sticky tape, fastened *securely* at each end with more sticky tape. (The sticky side must be *outside*, away from the ruler.)

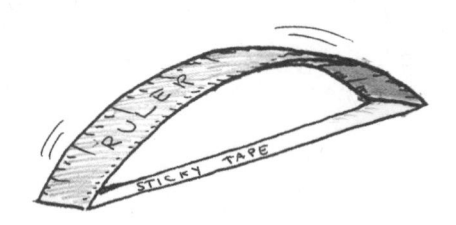

9 Hold the bum fiddle vertically in one hand, resting on the floor. Draw the 'bow' back and forth across the strip, at the part of the string near the balloon. You will need to practise getting good sounds by pressing harder or more gently with the bow. It will help to steady the balloon against one knee to stop the instrument twisting around as you bow it.

10 Your bum fiddle should now produce a note as you bow across the 'open' string, or pluck it with your finger. In the song, you need the note F. Find an F on chime bars or piano. Then play a matching F on your bum fiddle, either by pressing the string down on the wood with your finger, near the top, or by tying a piece of string round both string and stick, near the top. Move it up or down to get the right note.

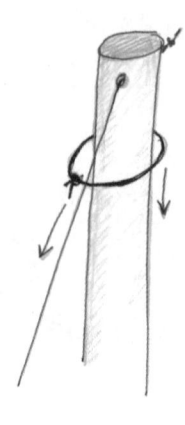

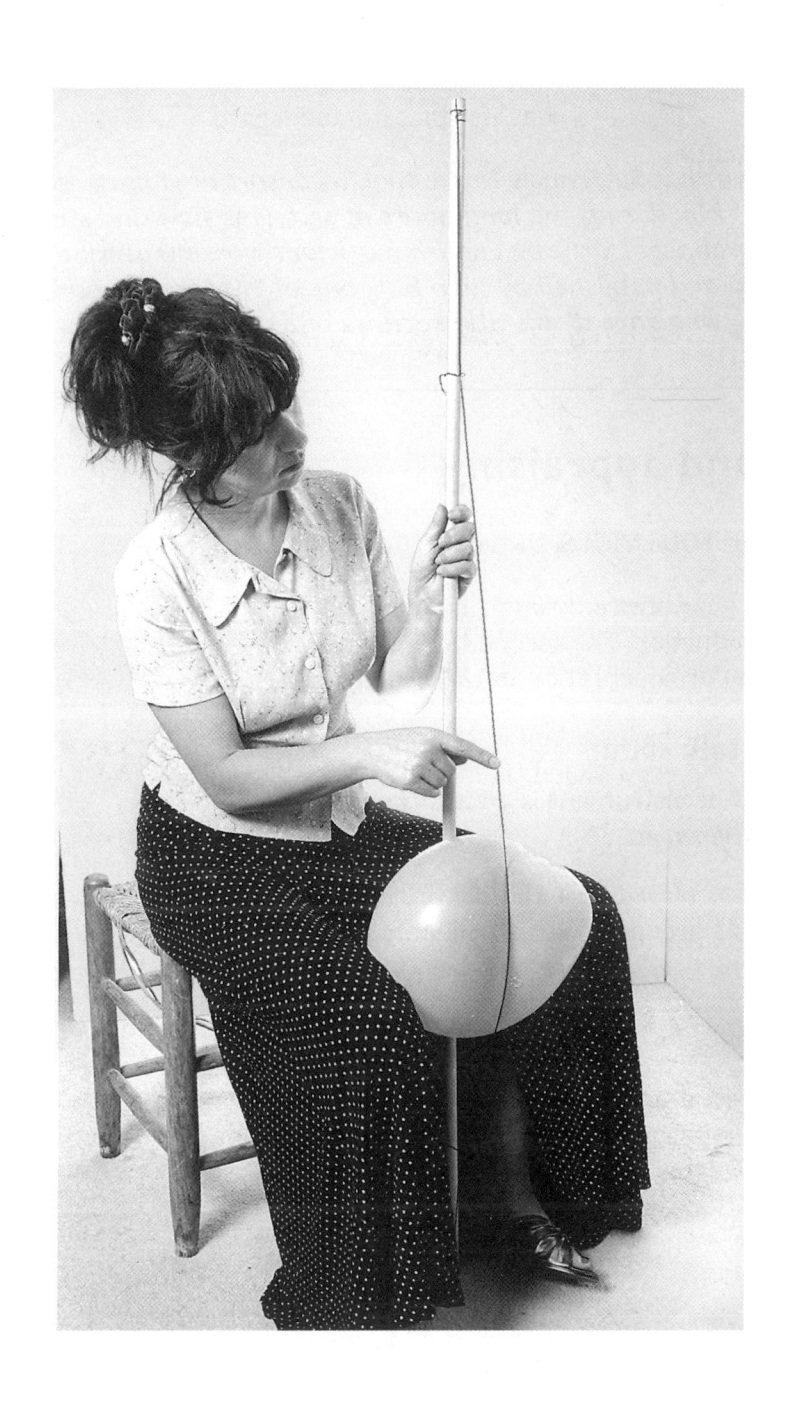

The completed bum fiddle

SIR FRANCIS DRAKE AND THE ARMADA

The Spanish Pavan

— CD Tracks 34 and 35 —

FOCUS ON:
A consort of viols
Playing staccato and legato

It is known that Sir Francis Drake took a consort of viols on board ship to entertain him during the long hours at sea. This slow and stately dance tune was probably learnt by English musicians working abroad. It was later rearranged and published by John Bull, one of Elizabeth's court composers, who gave it this title because of its Spanish origins.

Listening and appraising

You can hear: FOUR VIOLS, DRUM

The piece is heard twice through, starting with a drum introduction. The second time through, there is some ornamentation of the melody.

Things to talk about

1 What sort of instrument is a VIOL *(bowed, plucked, blown etc.)*?

2 This piece is played by a *consort of viols* - a consort is a group of like instruments, often of different sizes, playing together (also see *recorder consort* in *Queen Elizabeth's Almain*, page 66).

3 On the second time through you will hear that the viol player is 'decorating' the melody with some extra notes. This is a form of improvisation that was very popular in Tudor times (see *A Sailor's Dance for Catherine Parr*, page 48).

4 The drum plays what is known as a 'pavan rhythm'. This is the *long-short-short* rhythm you can hear all through. Pupils should gently clap this beat. You will notice that the viols reflect this rhythm, often playing the first part of each bar in a smooth and sustained way, followed by two shorter and lighter beats.

5 This dance music has a rather slow and stately feel. Compare it to the dance music used for *Queen Elizabeth's Almain* (page 66).

Now – let's make Tudor music!

RECORDERS 1/VIOLINS 1 (optional):
This part is suitable for more advanced instrumentalists (Grade 2 upwards). Start playing after the drum introduction. Make sure to follow the symbols for *legato* (smooth and flowing) and *staccato* (short and spikey).

RECORDERS 2/VIOLINS 2:
You could use the LEARNING TRACK (CD Track 35) first. Then, with the main track, start after the drum introduction. Make sure to follow the symbols for *legato* (smooth and flowing) and *stacato* (short and spikey).

CHIME BARS:
You need notes G, A and C (in ascending order). Play one note at the beginning of each bar all the way through. The letter-names above the notes are your part. Start after the drum introduction.

TAMBOURINES:
Use the LEARNING TRACK (CD Track 35) first. Listen to the rhythm of the tambourine *(long - short-short - long - long)* and copy it. Now play along with the main track, starting after the drum introduction.

DRUMS:
Use the drum introduction on the main track to pick up the rhythm *(long - short-short)*, clapping it gently first. Then ask pupils to choose a drum that most nearly resembles the sound of the drum on the CD track.

Other things to try

For ordinary poeple during the reign of Elizabeth, Spain was regarded as a hostile nation. How does this contrast with our awareness of Spain today as a partner in the European Union? Ask pupils to think of ways in which they might relate to Spanish culture nowadays (for example, Spanish omelettes, onions and paella; holidays in Benidorm; football celebrities and Carreras and Domingo of The Three Tenors).

Glossary of Instruments

Bagpipe (wind)
A rustic instrument often depicted in paintings of country life, the bagpipe combines a simple shepherd's pipe with the skin of a goat or sheep that forms the bag. Its great popularity through the ages is due to the ability to produce a continuous sound. Air is stored in the bag and let out or replenished gradually, so that the player need not take quick breaths as gaps in the tune allow. This feature makes it perfect for dance music, and economical, since a single player can supply both the melody and drone accompaniment.
   See: *Anne of Cleves' Dance, Robin Hood and the Poacher*

Bum Fiddle (stringed)
The bum fiddle's name probably derives from its shape. It is made from a pig's bladder that is inflated and placed on a simple stick of wood, with a string stretched tightly across to create a cleft. A peasant's instrument with a very limited range of notes, the bum fiddle is best used for playing easy rhythmic bass lines, rather like an early 'soap box' or 'bucket' bass.
   See: *The Invincible Armada*

Cittern (plucked strings)
After the lute, the cittern was the most popular plucked instrument in Tudor times. It was used chiefly for accompanying popular songs and rhythmical dance tunes, and its metal strings made a jangling, almost percussive sound. The cittern rarely played a melody by itself, more often being used to provide the chordal backing to a voice or melody instrument.
   See: *The Tale of Sir Eglamore and the Dragon, Tomorrow the Fox will come to Town*

Cornetto (wind)
The cornetto combines a mouthpiece typical of brass instruments, with the conical wooden tube and finger holes of the woodwind family. It can therefore blend well with the loud volume of a trumpet, or play as quietly as a recorder. The name means 'little horn'.
   See: *Fanfare*

Crumhorn (wind)
This is a reed-cap instrument in which the double reed (two broad pieces of cane fixed together) is hidden inside a wooden cap, and which is simply blown through a small hole at the top. Reflecting its curved shape, the name crumhorn derives from the German word *crum*, meaning 'crooked' (Old English *crump*). Henry VIII had a collection of 25 crumhorns, and they were almost always played together in a consort of instruments of various sizes.
   See: *Jane Seymour's Tune, Queen Elizabeth's Almain*

Curtal (wind)
The curtal is an ancestor of the modern bassoon. The CD features the bass version, which plays the lowest notes. It is actually twice as long as it looks. There are two tubes bored within one piece of wood with a U-bend at the bottom. The sound comes from the top.
   See: *The Tale of Sir Eglamore and the Dragon, Henry VIII's Song, Jane Seymour's Tune, Tomorrow the Fox will come to Town, Queen Elizabeth's Almain*

Drum (percussion)
Throughout the CD a selection of different-sized drums is featured. In Tudor times, the larger ones were sometimes attached to a belt, so that two sticks, or both hands, were free. Smaller drums were hit with one stick, hung over the arm, as in the pipe and tabor, or, as in the case of the tabor, hit with one or both hands.

Guitar (plucked strings)
The guitar of Tudor times was smaller and more delicate than the familiar Spanish guitar of today. It was strung with gut strings and often decorated, particularly around the sound hole in front, which might have an elaborate pattern made from parchment.
   See: *Katherine of Aragon's Song*

Harp (stringed)
Related to the Welsh or Irish folk harp, early harps were much smaller than their counterparts familiar from modern symphony orchestras. The early harp is held on the lap and plucked from either side with both hands. As with other bowed or plucked instruments, the strings are made of gut from sheep's intestines.
   See: *Robin Hood and the Poacher*

Hurdygurdy (keyboard)
The hurdygurdy combines features of bowed and keyboard instruments. It was sometimes known as a *vielle à roue* or 'wheel fiddle', as a rosined wheel sits in the body, beneath the strings. As the player turns the wheel from outside by means of a handle, all the strings resonate, providing a continuous sound. The melody is played by the left hand on a little keyboard which 'stops' the strings at different points to create different pitches. The hurdygurdy dates from the Middle Ages, and, due to its rasping sound and dance music associations was often portrayed in paintings in the hands of beggars and low-life characters. A rhythmic buzzing effect, the *trompette*, can be produced by an extra flick of the wheel.
   See: *Anne of Cleves' Dance, Robin Hood and the Poacher*

Lute (plucked strings)

The lute was the most important instrument of the Tudor period. The name comes from its Arabic ancestor, the *ud*. The lute's distinctive, rounded wooden back is made of thin strips of wood glued together. Another prominent feature is the peg box at the end of the neck, which is attached at an angle to the fingerboard. The strings are in pairs, and are plucked with the fingers. In the Elizabethan period the lute accompanied songs and also had a large repertoire of beautiful and virtuosic solo music.

   See: *When that I was a Little Tiny Boy, Anne Boleyn's Song, Jane Seymour's Tune*

Pipe and Tabor (wind and percussion)

The pipe and tabor are a kind of one man band, ideal for dance music. The drum gives the beat and the pipe plays the melody. The tabor, usually a small snare drum, is slung on the left-hand side of the body, often around the waist or over the left arm. The left hand holds the pipe, which has holes for two fingers and thumb. The right hand is free to beat the tabor. The pipe and tabor came into regular use at the time of the Medieval troubadours, and remained popular during Elizabethan times.

   See: *A Sailor's Dance for Catherine Parr*

Rauschpfeife (wind)

This is a loud instrument with a reed cap, similar to a crumhorn. It was chiefly used for music played out of doors.

   See: *Queen Elizabeth's Almain*

Rebec (stringed)

A small, pear-shaped bowed instrument, the rebec dates back to at least the Middle Ages. It can have any number of strings, from two to four or more, and its name derives from the Arabic *rebab*. The body, with its rounded back, was carved from a single piece of wood. Rebecs were not standardised, and came in various sizes and pitches. The smaller instruments were played resting in the armpit rather than under the chin.

   See: *Song of the Cutpurse, Henry VIII's Song, Catherine Howard's Song, Tomorrow the Fox will come to Town, Robin Hood and the Poacher, Queen Elizabeth's Almain*

Recorder (wind)

The most popular and versatile of early wind instruments, the recorder dates back to the 12th century. Like many other early instruments, it comes as part of a family of different sizes, covering a wide range of pitches: sopranino, descant, treble, tenor and bass.

   See: *Katherine of Aragon's Song, Queen Elizabeth's Almain, The Invincible Armada*

Sackbut (wind)
The name most probably derives from two French words, *saquer*, 'to pull', and *bouter*, 'to push'. As in our modern trombone, different notes are produced by pulling in and pushing out a length of brass tubing, lengthening and shortening the tube.
   See: *Fanfare*

Shawm (wind)
An ancestor of the oboe, the shawm is a cylindrical wooden pipe that has finger holes and flares out into a bell-shaped end. Like the rauschpfeife and crumhorn, it is played with a double reed. This is made of broad cane, and placed in the performer's mouth. On account of its loud tone, the shawm was often used by town bands and city waites for open air music.
   See: *Henry VIII's Song*

Viol (stringed)
Like many other Tudor instruments, viols were made in families, including treble, alto, tenor, bass and double bass, or violone. Viols are bowed like violins or cellos, the smaller members of the family being held on the lap.
   See: *Katherine of Aragon's Song, Jane Seymour's Song, Eliza is the Fairest Queen, Queen Elizabeth's Almain, The Spanish Pavan*

Violin (stringed)
Although the violin of the Tudor period looks similar to today's instrument, it was more lightly built, and had a flatter, slightly shorter fingerboard. The strings were made of gut.
   See: *The Tale of Sir Eglamore and the Dragon*

Virginals (keyboard)
This is a plucked keyboard instrument, in contrast to the piano, in which the strings are hit by a hammer. The box of the virginals is usually rectangular, with the strings running lengthwise, parallel to the keyboard. The player presses a note, operating a mechanical 'jack' that is equipped with a small plectrum made of quill. This rises and plucks the string. It is not possible to make contrasts either of dynamics or tone. Although the origin of the name may relate to Queen Elizabeth I, the 'Virgin Queen', who was a notable player on the instrument, it is more likely to refer in general to the young ladies often depicted playing the virginals in paintings of the period.
   See: *Eliza is the Fairest Queen, The Death of Queen Elizabeth*